Winter Sports

by

Heather and John Leigh

Macdonald Educational

Contents

Editor Kate Woodhouse
Assistant Editor Jim Miles
Design Peter Benoist
Production Philip Hughes
Picture Research Maggie Colbeck

First published 1975
Macdonald Educational
St Giles House
49-50 Poland Street
London W1

© Macdonald & Co.
(Publishers) Limited 1975

Made and printed by
Morrison and Gibb Ltd
London and Edinburgh

ISBN 0 356 05094 7

Katja and Knut Schubert from the
German Democratic Republic in a
perfectly balanced death spiral.

Early winter sports

From earliest times people have had to cope with ice and snow. It is possible that people have been skiing for as long as 5000 years. There are some carvings from the Stone Age, 4000 years ago. A ski god Ullr and goddess Undurrdis appear in Scandinavian mythology.

Skiing plays an important part in Norwegian history. In 1200 King Sverre of Norway used ski scouts in the battle of Illsen near Oslo. Six years later the king's son, Hakon Hakonson, was saved from an enemy by two skiers, who carried the boy across snow-covered mountains. To commemorate this event there is still a marathon ski race along this same route every year.

The earliest skis were made from wood and curved at both the front and the back. If one end broke while the skier was out hunting, the ski could be reversed. The ski was attached to the foot with a single strap across the toe. Instead of ski sticks people used one sharp pole. The pole could be used as both a spear for hunting and as a ski stick. Another type of skis was one long left ski and a short right ski, covered in skins. The largest known skis were used by a Norwegian gold miner in California over 100 years ago. They were about 3.5 metres (11 ft) long.

Although not a great deal is known about early skating, it is thought that the principle of skating was discovered long ago. The first skates that have been found were made from animal bone. These bones had a fairly sharp edge, which would have been quite good for skating on.

▲ This cave carving from Rødöyin, northern Norway is about 4000 years old. Skis were obviously invented a long time ago.

▶ Skates used to be made from the bone of large animals like the elk. Although they were not as efficient as steel skates they would get you across a frozen river or lake.

▶ A beautiful and ornate 19th-century skate belonging to Queen Victoria.

▼ In 1684 the river Thames in London froze over. This painting shows the fair which was held for several weeks, with oxen roasting over the fires.

Sledges, skis and skates

Although various kinds of skis and skates have existed for thousands of years, competitive sports on snow and ice are still relatively new.

Modern skiing starts with the invention of ski bindings in 1880 by Sondre Nordheim in Norway. In 1881 instructors from Telemark opened the first ski school. Soon after this modern skiing spread to other countries.

An Englishman, Arnold Lunn, first introduced downhill racing and the modern slalom. The word slalom comes from two Norwegian words, "sla" means slope and "lom" means trail. The first slalom race was in Murren, Switzerland, in 1922. 1924 was an important year for competitive skiing, the famous Kandahar Club was founded by Sir Arnold Lunn, the Fédération Internationale de Ski was founded in Oslo, and the first Winter Olympics were held in Chamonix, France.

Skating has been a popular sport for many hundreds of years. One of the most important people in the development of skating was an American named Jackson Haines. Before becoming a skater he was a ballroom dancer. He transformed the world of skating with his spectacular new technique, and was the inspiration of two other great performers, Ulrich Salchow and Axel Paulsen. The jumps that Salchow and Paulsen invented are named after them. Haines was the originator of the Viennese school of skating, which is so important to present-day international skating. The Vienna skating club was founded in 1867.

Transport and pleasure

Winter sports have a long history, arising first from necessity and then developing into sport. Snow and ice have a great fascination, people have always wanted to take advantage of these conditions by skating, tobogganing, skiing or any of the other winter sports.

▲ The winters in Russia are always extremely cold. In Leningrad, or St Petersburg as it was then called, people would live on the ice. The ice was frozen so thick that you could drive sledges across it without any fear of the ice cracking.

▼ Skating was a fashionable and favourite sport in France during the second half of the 19th century. The skaters would dance, skate in pairs or alone, and often men would push their wives along the ice in beautifully carved sledges.

▲ These people tobogganing in Canada at the end of the 19th century could be early bob sleighers. The toboggans themselves look fairly simple, but they probably went fairly fast.

▲ This game of bandy looks quite gentle compared with the present-day game. Bandy is similar to ice hockey, but it is played with a ball instead of a puck. The name of the game comes from the curved sticks or bandies.

▲ Snow shoes have been used for thousands of years as a method of walking over snow. In Canada there are races on snow shoes, which even include hurdling on them.

◄ About a hundred years ago, children in Switzerland used to go to school on toboggans and crude skis. The skis were made from the staves of beer barrels, and the ski stick would be just a long pole. The toboggans were similar to those used today.

Avalanches

Snow flakes form when the water vapour in clouds condenses at a temperature below freezing point (0°C 32°F). The flakes are made up of snow crystals. Although each crystal is different from the next, each has six sides. It is the air temperature between the clouds and the earth that determines the shape of the flakes. At 0°C and above, more crystals stick together so the snow falls in large wet flakes to produce a thick heavy layer. If the temperature is lower the flakes are smaller which produces a more powdery layer of snow.

Once the snow has fallen rain, sun, wind or frost will affect the final condition of the ski slopes. Rain on new snow helps to form a good base for further snow. The sun melts the upper snow layer which freezes at night and forms a crust. Wind blows snow off ridges into gulleys where it collects in a claylike, windpacked mass. Frost produces light, powdery snow.

When snow makes roads and tracks impassable, the loose top layers are cleared with snow-ploughs. The snow-ploughs either push the snow aside or cut into it with large rotating blades. When the snow is deep, pistes and ski runs are prepared for the skiers by a piste machine which flattens the snow into a tightly-packed mass.

After heavy snow, or when the temperature rises, the upper layers of snow on the slopes can become loose and unstable. This snow will sometimes come crashing down in an avalanche. sweeping away anybody and anything in its path.

Danger in the snow

Avalanches are defined as a shifting of the snow cover over a distance greater than 50 metres (150 ft).

There are two main categories of avalanche. Firstly the "loose-snow" avalanche is caused when *either* dry *or* wet loosely-packed snow collects on steep slopes. Secondly, "slab avalanches" are both wet and dry. In this case whole slabs of packed snow break away and slide down the mountain. Both types of avalanche may be prevented by planting trees or placing barriers in the areas where they are liable to form.

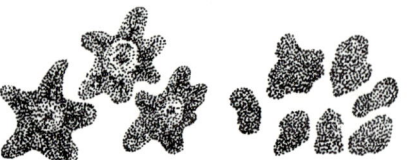

Snow crystals

A snowflake is a tiny six-sided crystal which grows as it falls through moist air. The spikes and plumes of the crystals interlock to make flakes.

After a short time on the ground, the flakes shrink and the points blunt and form grains which no longer stick together in a mass. In this condition, the snow is dangerous.

Later the grains settle and increase in size, as the original flakes disappear. The grains stick together and the snow becomes more stable.

▲ Trapped skiers must be found quickly before they freeze to death. Dogs are often used to sniff out the victim. St Bernards are the most famous rescue dogs in Europe, but they are now dying out.

▼ Another rescue method is for a line of people with steel poles to probe the snow very carefully to a depth of about 2 metres (6 ft). Although this method of rescue is fairly slow and painstaking, it is very thorough.

Powder
Airborne powder avalanches are the most devastating and fatal of all avalanches. New loose snow builds up on a slope, then the snow begins to slide. These avalanches can reach speeds of up to 350 kph (220 mph).

Wet avalanche
Wet loose-snow avalanches form mainly in spring when the snow is soaked with water. This weakens the snow structure so that it can slide. These avalanches move about 20 kph (15 mph) and set solid when they stop.

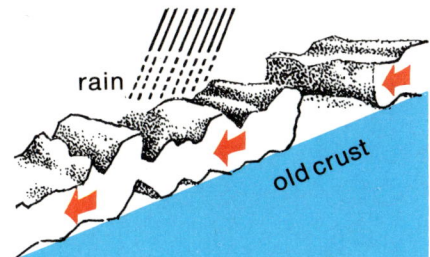

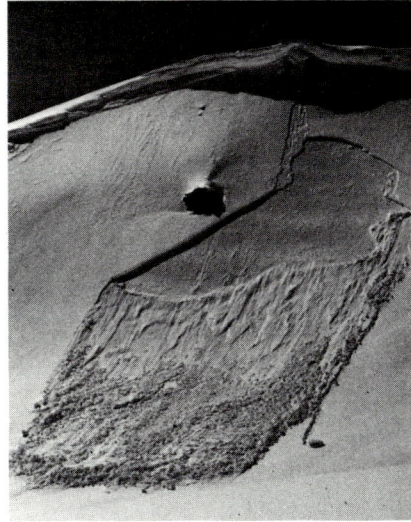

Wind slab
The wind packs the snow in a firm mass. This slab may not stick to the old surface below it, so a gap forms. With the slightest pressure, the slab breaks away and slides down the mountain, breaking up as it goes.

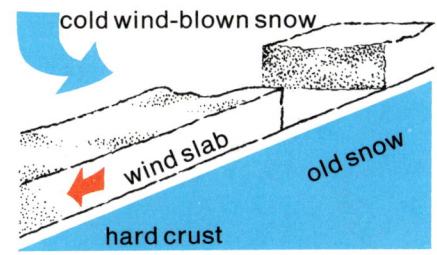

What to do in an avalanche
If an avalanche breaks and it is not possible to ski out of the way, get rid of your skis and sticks as fast as possible. Try to swim, using both your arms and legs, against the flow of the snow, as this will help you to stay on top. Keep your mouth firmly closed to stop powdered snow entering your lungs. As the avalanche slows down wrap your arms around your face. This makes a breathing space under the snow. When the avalanche stops try to escape. Do not panic, but conserve oxygen, so that you will be alive when rescue arrives. If you are skiing with a group, they will be searching the area to see if there is any sign of you before going for help.

Types of skiing and skis

Skiing can be divided into two distinct groups, the cross-country, or Nordic, and the downhill, or Alpine.

For many years the people of Norway and Sweden have used skis to travel over their snowy, rolling, wooded countryside. The present-day Nordic skiing has developed from this essential method of transport. It is really a cross-country walk on skis, where you take rhythmical, gliding steps. Your skis are light and relatively narrow, and your foot is attached to the ski only at the toe. There are far fewer turns in Nordic skiing than in Alpine skiing. Nordic skiing is also called *Langlauf*, or long run, in German, and *ski de fond*, or long-distance skiing, in French.

Alpine skiing is mainly fast downhill runs with many turns. The skis are heavier and wider than Nordic skis, the boot is bound to the ski at the heel as well as the toe, and the boot itself is larger than the Nordic boot so that it supports the ankle.

Nordic skiing has grown in popularity in recent years, particularly in Canada. It is less expensive than Alpine skiing. The main saving is in the cost of the lifts, which you do not need for this type of skiing.

Alpine skiing is taught in three ways: Austrian, French and Swiss. Each method differs slightly, and some have evolved new ways of teaching. The most important of these new ways of teaching is the short-ski method, which has become very popular in recent years.

On snow and grass

▼ The massed start of 10,000 skiers in the Engadine cross-country race in Switzerland. Whole families take part in this friendly competition.

Skiing techniques have to be adapted to the type of countryside you are in. The hills of the Scandinavian countries and parts of Canada are best suited to cross-country skiing, the steep slopes of the Alps and parts of North America to downhill runs. Skiing has now been adapted to snowless countryside in the form of grass skiing. Grass skiing can be done in any country, whether you have snow in winter or not. So now you can ski on hills or mountains, on snow or grass.

Cross-country
The equipment for cross-country skiing is considerably lighter than that used for Alpine skiing. The skis are made from light, laminated wood. They are much thinner and narrower than Alpine skis and do not usually have steel edges. The boots are similar to hiking boots, they are light and flexible without any special support for the ankles. Only the toe of the boot is attached to the binding, which itself is lighter than Alpine ski bindings. The ski poles are similar to Alpine sticks but are longer. They are usually about shoulder height.

You do not need to have any special clothes for cross-country skiing, as long as you are warm. Many people wear plus fours and long socks so that their feet are not hampered by trousers.

Bindings
For cross-country skiing a plate under the boot fits into pegs on the ski. There is a sprung toe clip which clamps down the front of the boot. The heel stays free.

Short skis

Short skis are becoming increasingly popular, particularly for beginners. They are easier to balance on than the usual length skis, and they are also easier to turn with. As these are the first things a beginner learns it is obviously quite sensible to start with short skis. They are best used on the hard snow of a piste or track, longer skis are better on soft or powdery snow. If you are a beginner, learning on nursery slopes with gentle gradients and hard snow, it is quite possible to use short skis without ski sticks. Beginners usually start with 100 cm (40 in) skis, then go on to 135 cm (55 in), 160 cm (65 in) and finally to normal length skis.

Tracked ski

Plain roller

Grass skis

Recently people have started to ski on grass during the snowless summer months and in countries with little or no snow in winter. Grass skis are nothing like snow skis. They are wheeled or tracked frames, similar to roller skates. The basic action is a mixture of skating and skiing. You flex your knees, push off as you would for skating and ski down the slope. You also have sticks to help your balance.

Wheeled ski

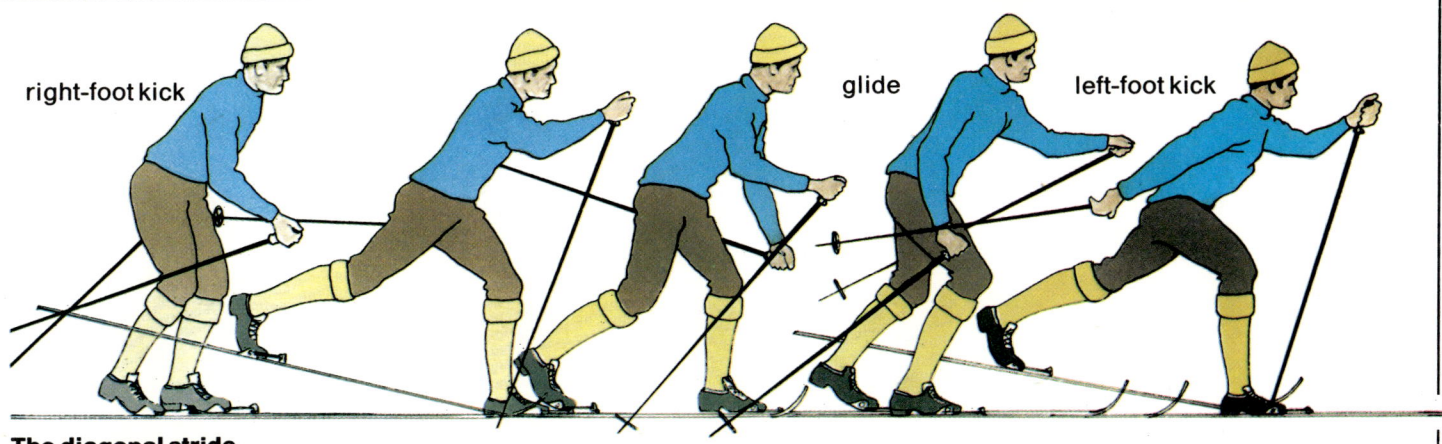

right-foot kick   glide   left-foot kick

The diagonal stride

The basis of the Nordic diagonal stride, whether for racing or pleasure, is a smooth coordination of movements between your arms and legs. It is very like walking. You flex your knees slightly and push off with your right foot and right pole so that your left foot glides forward. Push off with your left foot and pole and your right foot will glide forward. Your weight is transferred from ski to ski. As these movements are increased for racing, the pushing foot will tend to leave the snow more so that the glide is longer and faster.

Clothes and equipment

What you will need

It is very important to have the correct clothes and equipment when you go skiing. Your boots should fit comfortably and your skis should be the correct length to ensure that you ski as well as possible.

You will need some suitable clothes to go skiing, most of which can be worn during the winter at home as well. All the equipment can be hired at home or at the resort.

The essential clothes are snow-proof trousers, an anorak, thick sweaters, socks and gloves. You will be much warmer if you wear several thin layers of clothing rather than one thick layer. Several layers of clothes trap several layers of warm air, which obviously keeps you warmer than one layer of warm air. Many ski clothes are made of padded, nylon quilting, which is one of the warmest materials. People in very cold countries like the Soviet Union and China have worn cotton or silk padded clothes for hundreds of years.

Ski boots were originally made of leather, but you will probably find that the boots you hire are plastic. Plastic boots are very strong and give your ankle firm support.

Skis used to be made of wood, now they are usually fibreglass or metal. Ski sticks are made from the same materials. All makes of skis, ski boots and ski sticks vary slightly, but basically they are the same.

When you go into a ski shop you will be confronted with a huge variety of skiing clothes and equipment. As long as you are equipped with the essentials shown on this page and remember that you must keep warm and dry, the choice of clothes and equipment is your own.

Choosing your skis

To choose the correct length of skis for your height the skis should be at eye level. Some beginners learn on short skis, these should reach waist height.

Skis are made with a foam plastic core which is encased by fibreglass or metal. There is a groove down the centre of the sole so that the skis run straight. The curved tips make it easier to run over bumps. Short skis turn more easily and are therefore better for beginners.

Bindings

Boots are attached to the ski with bindings. These are set so that the boot will be released from the ski if you fall badly. One of the most popular bindings has a swivel toe piece with a separate heel unit. When you fall your toe swivels and the heel unit opens. A teflon pad helps the toe swivel off the ski. A loose ski travelling down a mountain can be lethal, so the ski is permanently attached to your leg with a loose-fitting strap.

Hats
Your ears will become very cold without a hat. The type shown here is a popular one. Ear muffs or a head band are also suitable.

Jackets and jerseys
Your anorak should zip up to the neck to keep out the cold. Underneath people wear cotton shirts and jerseys for extra warmth. Anoraks are sold in a great variety of colours and patterns.

Bumbag
A bumbag is a small waterproof bag which you wear round your waist to carry extras.

Trousers
Trousers should be snow and windproof. They are made of the same material as anoraks, often to match. They should cover your boots, but not be too long so that they interfere with your clips and bindings.

Ski sticks
To choose the correct length ski sticks in the shop your hand should be just above waist level. To hold the stick properly you put your hand through the loop so that the sticks hang from your wrist, and then you grip the handle. The sticks help you to balance and are useful when you are climbing and making some turns. The plastic disc or basket at the end of the stick is to stop it from sinking in to the snow.

Goggles
Tinted goggles protect your eyes from the glare of the sun reflected on the snow.

Socks
It is best to have an inner, thin pair of socks and an outer thick pair.

Gloves
Gloves should be padded on the back to protect your hands if you fall. The elastic cuffs keep out the cold.

Wax
Wax rubbed on to the under side of your skis will make them go faster or slower according to the condition of the snow.

Suntan lotion
The sun can be very strong at high altitudes, so it is wise to protect yourself.

Fitting your boots
Most boots are made of rigid plastic, lined with foam plastic. It is essential that they should fit comfortably and correctly. Your heel and ankle should be held firmly, but your toes should be free to move. There is a hinge on the ankle so that your ankle can move. The boots are closed with adjustable clips, not laces. The soles are thick, flat and rigid.

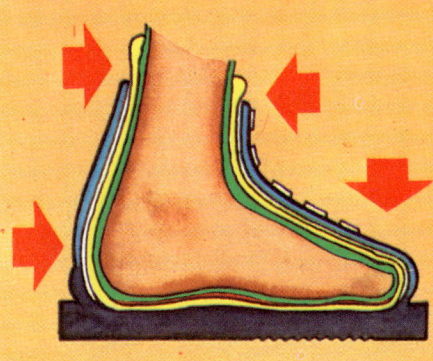

The basic steps

Skiing is an extremely enjoyable and exhilarating sport. As with any sport there are various aspects of it that you have to master before you can really enjoy it. All the movements shown on this page are the basic essentials, once you can do these you are on the way to becoming a competent skier.

When you first ski down a gentle slope you will probably find that you either fall over backwards, or that when you stop you over-balance forwards. The combination of skis and a slope under your feet means that the way you balance will be different from usual. Walking on your skis is excellent practice for your balance, as is kick turning. When you can balance on your skis without difficulty you should be able to complete the basic steps shown on this page.

As a beginner it is a very good idea to go to ski school. Qualified instructors will demonstrate and teach you all the basic steps and help you to correct any of your faults. There are several different ways of teaching skiing. In some countries beginners are taught on short skis, going on to longer and longer skis as they become more confident.

When you are ready to go out on your first run you should go out with an experienced skier in case you get into difficulties. You should always keep to a marked track or piste which has been specially prepared for skiers, as there should be no natural hazard on these.

Starting on skis

All the steps here are the basic ones for a beginner. It is best to try to be able to do these easily before moving on to more advanced steps. Before you go on the ski slope always check your equipment and ensure that your boots are correctly fitted into the bindings.

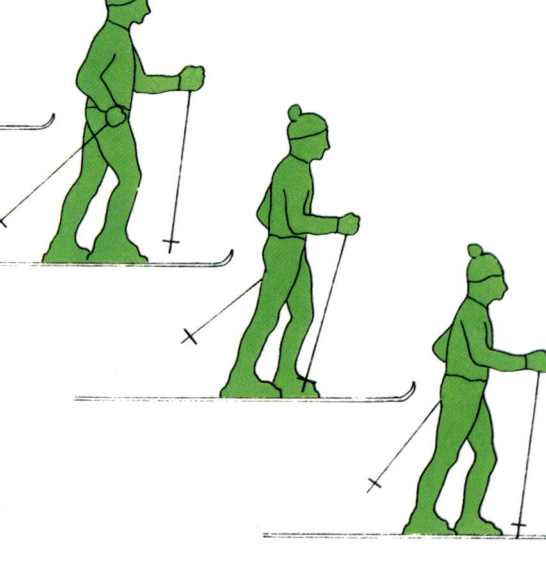

▲ These three people show the way in which you should get up from a fall. Always make sure that your skis are parallel and below you on the hill before you get up.

Walking
Walking helps you to get used to the feel of your skis. Start by standing on one foot and raising and lowering the other a few times keeping your ski parallel with the ground. When you have done this with both feet stand with your skis together, knees flexed and bend slightly forward. With your weight on the right ski slide your left foot forwards and push with your right stick, and then repeat this with the other foot.

Side stepping
Side stepping is one of the ways of climbing on skis. You place your skis at right angles to the hill so that they cannot run backwards or forwards. With your weight on the lower ski lift the upper ski to take a short step sideways edging your ski into the snow. At the same time move your upper stick above your upper foot. Then transfer your weight to the upper foot and step up with the lower ski, following and balancing with the lower stick.

Kick turn

Before you start your skis should be parallel. To make a right turn put the right stick by the rear of the right ski and the left stick by the front of the left ski. Kick your right leg up so that the tip is resting in the snow.

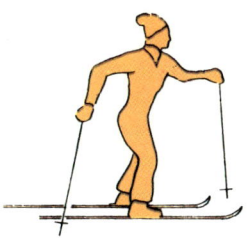

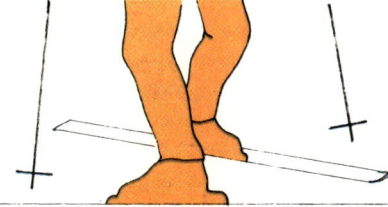

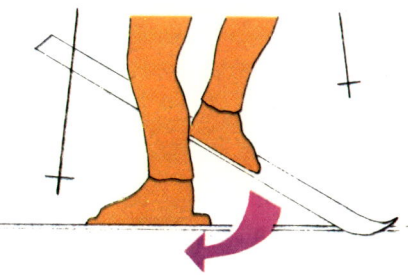

Swing your leg so that the right ski falls parallel but reverse to the left ski. Using your sticks as supports swing the left ski round so that it is parallel to the right ski. When you are on a slope turn first on the lower ski, swinging out over the slope.

Straight running

Straight downhill running, sometimes called *schussing,* is one of the most delightful parts of skiing. It is best to try downhill running first on a gentle slope with a flat end. Start with your skis parallel with one ski slightly ahead of the other. Your knees should be flexed and the upper part of your body at right angles to the skis. Your weight should be on the balls of your feet, with slightly more on the trailing ski. Your arms should be as low as possible with the sticks just lifted clear of the snow. Your knees are shock absorbers, they should bend more as you go over bumps. Remember to relax all the time.

Snowplough stop

This stop is for slowing down as well as stopping. You press your weight on the inside edges of the skis and at the same time press your heels outwards to form a V. Your knees should be bent, your body at right angles to the skis and your arms and sticks held down by your side. The harder the pressure on the inner edges and the wider the V, the faster the stop.

Snowplough turn

This starts from the snowplough stop position. By bending your body to put extra weight on one of the skis you will start to turn in the direction of that ski.

Traverse

The traverse is straight running diagonally across a slope. You keep your skis close together and parallel and edged into the hill. The upper ski should be in front of the lower, with your weight concentrated on the lower ski. Your uphill shoulder and hip should be slightly forwards, knees bent and arms at your sides with the sticks clear of the snow. As this running position is the basis of many advanced turns you should practise it carefully.

Advanced techniques
Confidence in christies

Once you have mastered the basic steps there are a number of more advanced steps that will widen the scope of your skiing. With these steps you should be able to travel over more difficult ground without any trouble. The steps shown here are some of the more advanced steps.

Side slipping

The side slip is the basis for the faster skid turns used by more advanced skiers, but it is important to master the technique at this stage. The side slip is good for losing height rapidly.

To side slip, lean outwards away from the mountain, and with your skis close together put the upper ski slightly in front of the lower one. Your weight should be spread evenly from heel to toe and your arms held as low as possible with the sticks clear of the snow. Release the pressure on the upper edges of the skis, which, as they are flattened against the slope, will slip sideways.

Uphill christie

Starting from the traverse position you should unweight your skis so that they begin to move sideways. Then flex your knees, bringing your weight down on to the heel of your lower ski. Reapplying your weight will push your heels downhill. The combination of this movement and the forward motion of the traverse will make your skis slip uphill.

Unweighting

As unweighting the skis is an important part of the fast parallel christie turn, you should practise it before actually attempting the full turn. Start from the traverse position, with your body leaning outwards and the upper ski leading the lower ski with most of the weight on the lower ski. Hold your arms as low as possible with the sticks clear of the snow, and flex your knees. To unweight, straighten your knees, so that your body weight moves upwards and lightens the pressure of the ski on the snow. The skis may now move sideways across the snow. Flex your knees again and the pressure of the ski on the snow is restored. If you unweight quickly your skis may leave the snow.

Stem christie

From the traverse position with your weight on the lower ski and your body leaning outwards, move your upper ski into the snowplough position. Then transfer your weight on to the upper ski, straighten your legs and bring the lighter ski parallel to the weighted ski. Bend your legs and your skis will slide round to traverse in the opposite direction.

Parallel christie

The parallel christie is a fast turn which can be done on steep slopes. It differs from the stem christie in that the skis are kept parallel throughout the turn. At the start of a parallel christie turn, your knees are flexed in the traverse or straight running position, with the weight on the trailing ski. You then unweight the skis, advance the trailing ski and transfer your weight to the other ski, this pushes the ends of the skis sideways to start the turn. This turn is easier at speed.

Skiing without snow

Skiing uses muscles all over your body, muscles that you do not usually use in everyday life. To prepare yourself for this it is a good idea if possible, to do some pre-ski training.

Pre-ski training can be divided up into three groups. Firstly, preparing your muscles for the extra work they will be doing; secondly, learning about the equipment and basic techniques before you reach the ski slopes; and, thirdly, practising the more advanced techniques.

If you are fairly active you should not find it difficult to exercise the muscles you will use for skiing. When you ski it is your whole body, not just your leg muscles that take the strain, so you must do more than just leg exercises. Walking upstairs with your toes on the edge of the stairs, press ups, knee bends, all help exercise your muscles. It is best to start the exercises gradually about two months before you leave. If you only start at the last moment too vigorously you may strain a muscle!

Skiing on artificial slopes is one of the best ways to practise. Artificial slopes are very different from the real thing, but they give you a good idea of the problem of balance, and of the different equipment you will be using. On the slopes you can practise all the basic and more advanced techniques.

Grass skiing is another useful preparation. The technique is different from snow skiing, but it still gives you a good impression of snow skiing. One advantage of grass skiing is that you can practise all the year round.

The dry slope

Skiing on artificial slopes is an enjoyable sport even if you are not going to ski on snow. If you are going for a skiing holiday artificial slopes are very good practice before you go.

▲ This artificial ski slope is made from nylon bristles in circles of about 12 cm (5 in) in diameter. On some artificial slopes the bristles are sometimes not very slippery, so the skiers have to walk through a tray of oil to lubricate their skis. This can be quite an advantage to a beginner who will not go down a slope too fast. Most artificial slopes are made of similar materials.

▼ The mogulslope is a very different type of artificial slope. The skier stands in the same place while a machine moves the ground under the skier's feet. You wear short skis on the mogulslope. You can practise any type of step on the mogulslope, which makes it a very good system for the more advanced skiers. It also has the advantage of being an indoor slope which can be used in all weathers.

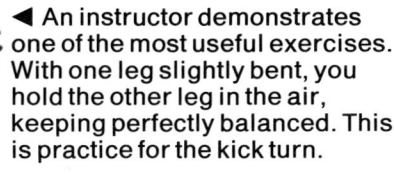

◄ An instructor demonstrates one of the most useful exercises. With one leg slightly bent, you hold the other leg in the air, keeping perfectly balanced. This is practice for the kick turn.

► The younger you learn the easier it is to ski. These children are learning without sticks at the moment to accustom themselves to the different balance you need.

▲ A general view of the artificial slope shows the great variety of runs you can do. The boy in the foreground is doing a straight run down a steep slope.

▲ The snowplough stop is one of the first steps you learn. One of the instructors shows a young boy how to do one. As the slope here is quite gentle it is quite easy to teach people these basic techniques.

◄ The bollards on the slope represent small slopes you would have to go round using the snowplough turn on the ski slopes. In the background you can see a very steep slope on which the more advanced skiers practise.

► Artificial slopes have as many bumps and slopes as a snow slope. You can practise how you have to think and act quickly to deal with these problems. One disadvantage of artificial slopes is that they are rather hard to fall on.

The artistry and speed of the ski jumper's flight through the air.

Italy's Gustavo Thoeni demonstrates his nerve and skill in the slalom.

Jumping and downhill *Grace and daring*

The ski village

Winter sports resorts vary from the large sophisticated village or town accessible by road, rail or air, to the small hamlet of a small collection of houses and one or two hotels which can be reached only by mountain railway.

Whatever the size of the resort they all lie in a mountainous region which has a reasonable snow fall and a holiday season of at least three months. From the village there will be ski lifts and chair lifts for longer rises, and cable and funicular cars for the higher peaks. These all give the village a range of ski slopes from almost flat ground for beginners to very steep slopes for the experts. Although some villages are better for beginners and others for more advanced skiers, most villages have possibilities for all skiers.

Many ski villages have an individual charm and character. There may be older houses and hotels clustered around the church, with the newer buildings on the outskirts. In many resorts cars are banned. The larger villages have all the usual facilities like a bank and post office, as well as the special sports and tourists shops and ski school for the visiting skiers.

Skiing is often only one of the many things you can do in these villages. There may be an ice rink for skating, curling and ice hockey, or a special toboggan run. You can usually find paths for walking to enjoy the marvellous scenery. For the evening there are bars, cafes, discotheques, and possibly a bowling alley and a cinema.

Sport and entertainment

You can discover all the facilities a village has to offer from the official information bureau. The bureau also issues weather forecasts and ski-run information. They will tell you how to buy season tickets for the lifts and coupons for the ski school.

funicular

skating rink

curling rink

T-bar lift

When you get on to a ski lift your knees should be slightly bent. Your arm nearest the T-bar steadies the bar while the cable takes the strain. You must not sit down on the bar, just let it pull you up. Swing the bar clear when you want to get off.

cable car

ski jump

bobsleigh run

drag lift

nursery slopes

Advanced skiers on the upper slopes may find large areas of undisturbed powder snow. It can be very exciting to be the first person to ski across this snow. At this height the weather can change very quickly, so you have to take care.

On the middle slopes there are wide, prepared pistes which vary in difficulty. In spells of fine weather there may be bare and icy patches. As many skiers use these slopes there are regular patrols in case of accidents.

Nearer the village the slopes are gentler. The ski-school classes work on these slopes practising the various steps. There are often long queues here for the ski lifts up to the higher slopes.

Competitive skiing

Competitive skiing is often breathtaking to watch. The skiers seem to fly down the slopes or through the air at a quite terrific speed. The Winter Olympics are the most important of the competitive events. They are held every four years, the winter before the main Olympics. During the four years between there are many other competitions that are held all over the world.

The skiing events in the Winter Olympics are divided between Nordic and Alpine skiing. The Nordic events are jumping, cross-country skiing, relay, biathlon and Nordic combined. All these events test the endurance, strength and judgement of the skier. Jumping is over a marked course from a particular point. For the cross-country skiing the competitor has to ski over a marked track of natural terrain, covering uphill, downhill and flat conditions. The relay is a variation on the cross-country racing involving a team of skiers. The biathlon combines cross-country skiing with rifle shooting and the Nordic combined includes cross-country and jumping.

The Alpine events are downhill racing, slalom, giant slalom and the Alpine combination. For the downhill the skiers must go down a marked difficult piste as fast as possible, and for the slalom descend a twisting course, again as fast as possible. The giant slalom combines the downhill and slalom, the Alpine combination is a downhill race and a slalom race. These races are all incredibly fast so the skiers must have both skill and nerve to complete the courses.

Aiming for the best

Competitive skiing is extremely exciting for the spectator. The speed of the skiers, the beauty of the snow against the brilliant blue sky and the difficulty of the events make compulsive watching.

▶ This view from the top of a ski jump gives you a good idea of what you see, and perhaps feel, before you set off.

Jumping
Skis for jumping are longer, wider and heavier than ordinary skis. They do not have steel edges, but have three grooves on the bottom instead of one to help the skier to steer. The snow on the jump must be hard and smooth from start to finish.

The jumper skis off on the in-run in a crouched position with his arms forward and down. When he reaches the take off, by which time he will be travelling very fast, he straightens his legs and leans forwards with his arms at his sides. The jumper's body is almost parallel to his skis. Throughout the jump the skis should be parallel. As he lands the jumper keeps his balance by bending the knees and arms. The jumps are judged on precision, style and distance.

The weather is an important factor in ski jumping. If the wind is very strong jumpers can be blown off course to fall and injure themselves badly.

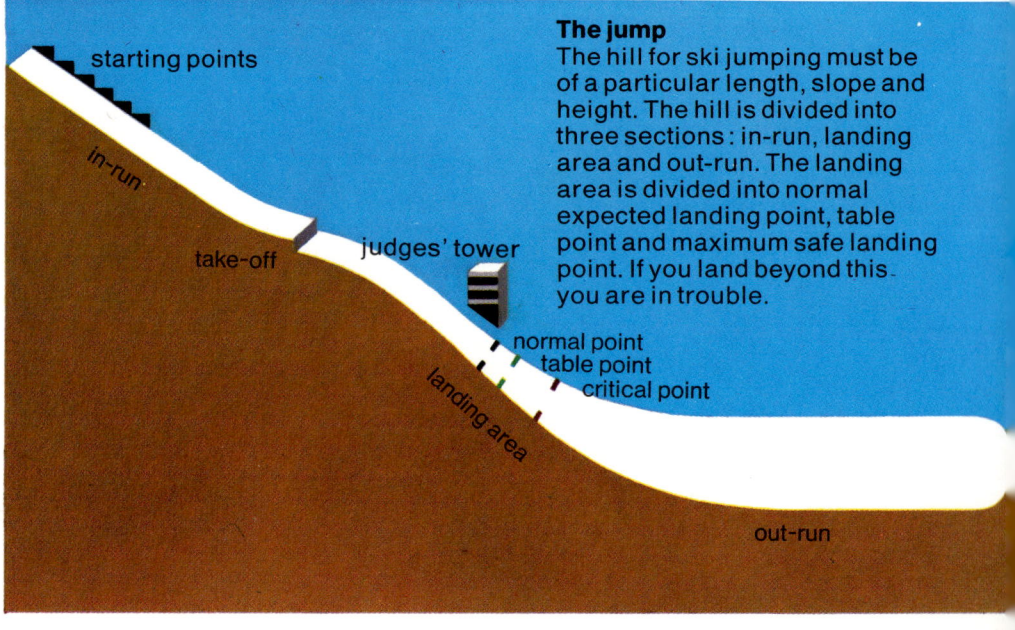

starting points

in-run

take-off

judges' tower

normal point
table point
critical point

landing area

out-run

The jump
The hill for ski jumping must be of a particular length, slope and height. The hill is divided into three sections: in-run, landing area and out-run. The landing area is divided into normal expected landing point, table point and maximum safe landing point. If you land beyond this you are in trouble.

Downhill

Downhill racing is the fastest and one of the most dangerous of competitive skiing events. Skiers reach speeds of up to 130 kph (80 mph) as they race down the course. The skiers set off separately and their run is timed, the one with the fastest time wins.

Men's courses have a drop of 850–1000 m (2800–3300 ft) and women's courses 400–700 m (1300–2300 ft). The course is marked with flags along each side and there are control gates in certain places to limit the speed of the racers. The course is chosen so that the run can be completed without having to use ski sticks. The course must not have any sharp ridges or obstructions which would force the competitors to leave the ground for more than a short time.

◄ The sleek powerful lines of Kim Mumford (USA) as he speeds towards the finish of a downhill race.

Biathlon

The biathlon is a combination of cross-country skiing and rifle shooting. The length of the course is usually 20 km (12½ miles). The competitors have to cover five 4 km sprints, shooting at targets at the end of the first four sprints. Five shots are fired at each target from 150 m (492 ft). Two shots are fired at a larger target lying down, and two fired standing at a smaller target. For each shot missed two minutes are added to the total race time, shots that hit the outer target ring add one minute. The competitor completing the course in the shortest time wins.

←35 cm→

← 45 cm →

Slalom

The slalom is a downhill race which follows a twisting course marked by pairs of flags and poles called gates. There are four types of gate: open, closed, hairpin and combination. In men's races there are between 55 and 75 gates and in women's between 40 and 60. The racers begin from a starting gate, and as in the downhill, they set off separately, their time is recorded, and the fastest skier is the winner. The competitors have to combine speed with turning skill and excellent judgement.

starting gate

open gates

closed gates

hairpin

combination

Safety and sense

Winter sports, like any other sports, have their rules and regulations which should be obeyed for your own and other people's safety. If you take care and think before you do anything you should not be involved in any accidents.

There is a code of rules for skiers which covers such points as: the slower skier has the right of way, give way to a beginner, if you are overtaking avoid the skier below or beyond you. A skier should always be sure to read all the signs and markers on the pistes and lift systems. Inexperienced skiers should not ski in isolated areas alone, or continue to ski when they are tired in case they find themselves stranded.

The accident rescue service on the ski slopes is run by some of the best skiers. These people are able to ski down the steepest slopes, without sticks, carrying someone on a stretcher between them. They ski straight down many of the slopes that other people would zig-zag down. This service is sometimes called the "bloodwagon".

The rules for skating are not as clearly set out as they are for skiing. One of the most important for outdoor skaters is to be sure that the ice will hold you. Falling through ice can be very serious if the pond is deep. Again, you should look out for beginners and not let your actions upset and disturb them.

Driving a toboggan you should take care not to let it go too fast if there are a lot of people around. You should make sure you will be able to stop easily, especially if you have any passengers.

Look before you leap

These are some of the things you must never do if you, and people around you, are to ski safely and comfortably. Although the accident rescue service is very good and efficient, with care you can avoid having to use them.

Don't do too many exercises just before you leave for your skiing holiday, you could pull a muscle and not be able to ski.

Don't wear too many clothes, long scarves can be very dangerous.

Be sure that you know how to contact the accident rescue service.

Skating can be a dangerous sport if you behave thoughtlessly. The blades on skates are extremely sharp and could hurt someone very badly if they are not properly used. Good skaters should always remember that learners may not be able to stop when they want to stop.

Skating blades are very sharp, they should always be covered when they aren't being used.

Never skate so fast that you can't stop when you want to stop.

Don't walk across a specially prepared piste without your skis on. Someone's ski may go into one of the holes you have made.

Be sure to carry your skis correctly, you could knock someone out with them.

Thin ice
Skating on thin ice is very dangerous. If the water is deep and cold you could drown. To rescue somebody don't walk on the ice towards them as you will fall in. Get a ladder or planks which will spread your weight and edge your way out to them.

Some common warning signs

Runs cross

Danger

Caution
Run narrows

Run crosses railway

closed
barré
gesperrt
chiuso

closed
barré
gesperrt
chiuso

Piste maker

Local danger of snow slabs
Danger local de plaques de neige
Lokale Schneebrettgefahr
Pericolo locale di lastre di neve

Temporary danger

Danger of avalanches
Danger d'avalanches
Pericolo di valanghe
Lawinengefahr

Barriers

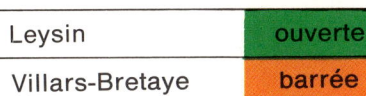

| Leysin | ouverte |
| Villars-Bretaye | barrée |

These are some of the signs you will see round a ski resort. Be sure that you know exactly what they mean before you go out as they are important.

Easy descent

Moderate descent

Difficult descent

SOS telephone

First aid

Accident service

Unusual winter sports

Recently a number of very elaborate winter sports have developed from skating, skiing and tobogganing. Some are extremely difficult and require a great deal of skill, like hot-dogging, but others, like ski-bobbing, are fairly easy. These new sports mean that more people can now enjoy the snow and ice, whether they are taking part or just watching as spectators.

If you are lucky enough to live somewhere where it snows in winter you will know the endless fun that snow can give. One of the most obvious things is snowballing, and also making snowmen and igloos from ice like the eskimos.

When rivers or lakes freeze over there are often parties and celebrations on the ice. An example of this is a ceremony that a town in Germany and another in Switzerland perform when the lake between them freezes over. There is a statue that they carry in a procession from one town to the other over the frozen lake. The statue then stays in that town until the lake freezes over another winter and the statue is taken back again, which may be 15 or more years away.

One of the newest winter sports is hot-dogging. For this you have to be an excellent skier. Some parts of it are similar to figure and pair skating except that it takes place on the snow with the competitor wearing skis. In the United States there are now large money prizes for these events. The competitors speed down a slope, take off from a short ramp and do twirls, loops and somersaults in the air.

Fun in the snow

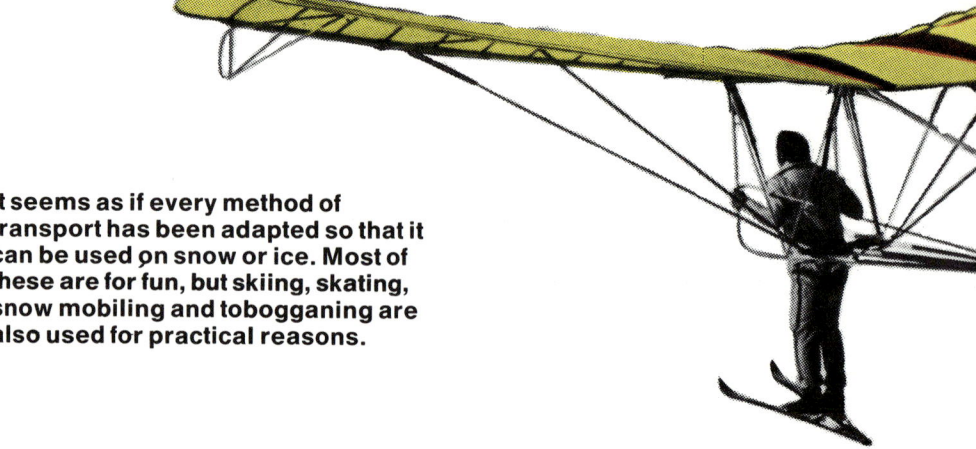

It seems as if every method of transport has been adapted so that it can be used on snow or ice. Most of these are for fun, but skiing, skating, snow mobiling and tobogganing are also used for practical reasons.

▼ Horse-drawn sleigh rides were one of the first winter sports. Many village winter festivals were celebrated by processions of sleighs with everyone dressed in national costume.

▲ Ski vol is a new sport. The skier is strapped to a glider made of lightweight material with a wingspan of about 16 metres (48 ft). The glider works just as an ordinary glider does.

► A ski bob is like a wooden or metal bicycle with skis instead of wheels. It is very easy to ride and an enjoyable way of coming down a mountain if you cannot ski very well. You wear small skis on your feet to help braking and balancing. Children can be carried on the crossbar, which makes ski bobs useful for parents. On a ski bob you can ride down a mountain as quickly or slowly as you like.

▼ Hot-dogging is a new form of free-style skiing that is particularly popular in North America. It is divided into three sections: aerials, ballet and the mogul run. The aerials are a downhill run with three acrobatic jumps. For the ballet section the competitor skis down a slope to music making figures and turns like figure skating. The mogul run is a downhill run with huge moguls, or bumps, on which the skier performs acrobatics.

▲ Ice boating is very popular in North America. The boats are made like catamarans with four points holding the skates. The mast is 5 metres (16 ft) high with 55 square metres (600 sq. ft) of sail.

▼ Ski-jøring, or ski-towing, is when the skier is towed over a flat track by one or more horses. In many large resorts there are organized races. Skiers are sometimes towed by cars, motor cycles or aircraft.

The art of skating *Precision and harmony*

Tension and determination show on this ice racer's face as he leans into the bend.

▲ Dorothy Hammill (USA) in the dramatic butterfly jump.
▼ Ice-dancing champions Pakhomova and Gorchakov (USSR).

▲ World pair-skating champions Irina Rodnina and Alexander Zaitsev (USSR) doing a perfect lift.

Principles of skating

Indoor rinks have made skating an all-year-round sport. You can enjoy it at different levels; simply for fun, for competition or as a profession.

The main expense is a pair of skates which can be hired quite cheaply. In time it is better to buy your own skating boots since they will fit better than hired ones. Buy them half a size smaller than your usual shoe size. The ankle should have firm support but the toes must not be cramped. Undo the laces completely when you put your boots on and when you lace them up do so firmly at the ankle. Blades can be an expensive item and since there are different types of blade for different types of skating it is a good idea to get advice before buying them. They should be well looked after and reground from time to time. You will not need any special clothes for skating, but a rink can often be quite cold so it is a good idea to wear a thick jersey.

Ice skating offers great variety, from the occasional visit to the local rink on Saturday afternoons to the glittering world of ice pantomimes. If you are reasonably fit and have an average sense of balance you can quickly develop enough proficiency to enjoy the sensation of gliding effortlessly over the ice. If you decide you want to go beyond this there are great challenges and much hard work ahead. You must learn the precision of the compulsory figures, and how to do turning leaps in the air. But at whatever level you skate, and wherever you skate, there will be lots of fun.

The knife edge

The one necessary piece of equipment is the skating boot and blade. Often people complain that they are finding skating too difficult because of their weak ankles. Although the trouble is usually due to ill-fitting boots there are ways you can strengthen your ankles.

▲ The strong and graceful John Curry, one of the world's most promising male figure skaters. Born in Birmingham, he trained at Richmond and Denver. In the World Championship of 1975, he won the bronze medal.

teeth
edge
groove

Types of skates
For speed skating the blades are long and thin. Hockey blades are a little thicker but still designed for speed. Figure skates have many variations. To assist with jumps and spins the figure blade has a toe rake, whereas both hockey and speed skates are smoothly curved at the toe. The blades are fixed to the boot and are kept sharp by specialists.

Edges
The blade is hollow ground on the bottom to give two skating edges: the inside edge and the outside edge. Skating on an edge means the body leans over that edge to make a forward or backward movement in a curve.

The spin

Start to move slightly forwards or backwards. Now begin to turn.

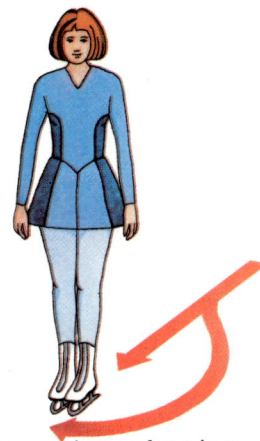

Lift both arms and your free leg. This starts the spin by throwing the body weight slightly off-centre.

The whole body goes into a wobbly spin which is steadied by bringing in the outstretched leg.

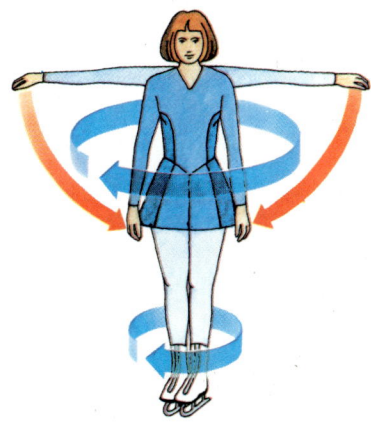

Bring your arms closer to your body. The further you bring them in the faster you will spin.

Exercises

You can do useful exercises both on and off the ice. Done for a short while each day these exercises will improve the muscles you need for controlled skating.

Ankles and calf

To strengthen the ankles and calf muscles stand with your toes on the edge of the stairs. Holding on to the rail, raise your heels up and down. Don't attempt this too vigorously. More important still, don't let your feet slip off the edge of the stairs. This could do you more harm than good.

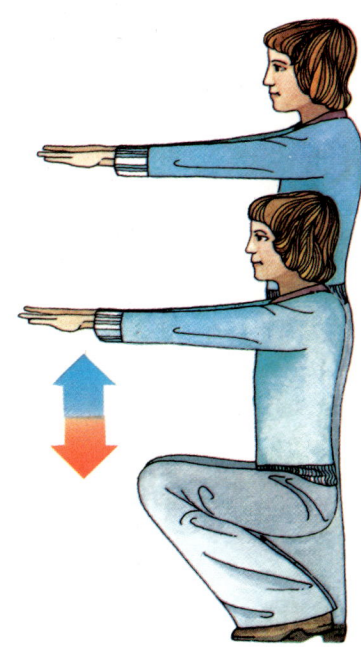

Legs and balance

Start from a "sleepwalker's" position—arms to the front, hands shoulder high and palms down. With your feet about 30 cm (1 ft) apart, squat until you are sitting on your heels, then come up slowly and repeat.

Thighs

To strengthen thighs, stand on the left leg and hold on to some support with the left hand. Raise your right leg to the front to a height of about 50cm (20 in) and hold it there for a few seconds. Swing the leg straight back and hold again. Do this several times then repeat with the other leg.

Falling and getting up

If you feel you are falling on the ice, try to sit down by bending your knees. Relax your muscles and don't put your hands on the ice. To get up get on your hands and knees, bring one foot between your hands and in line with your knee. Now bring the other foot forward. Take your hands off the ice, and straighten your knees. Keep your arms forward to help balance.

On the ice

When you first begin to skate, go if possible with a group of friends who can skate, but if you are on your own it is a good idea to arrange for a lesson from an instructor. Don't be discouraged if you fall at first. Indoor rinks have barriers which you can use for support if you need to. A crowded rink can be unnerving so try to go when it is quieter. It takes practice to acquire confidence, so don't worry about looking or feeling stupid at your first try. Besides—others will be too busy with their own skating.

Begin by watching other people skating to get an idea of the gliding movement. Make sure your boots fit well and that you have laced them up tightly since loose boots will make your ankles hurt. Clothes that are warm, but not too bulky are the most suitable.

Get used to the skates by walking for a while off the ice. When you step on the ice, do so slowly and carefully. Remember that at most rinks the skaters move in an anti-clockwise direction. You will not be popular if you go the other way. Bend your knees, relax and don't lean backwards. Don't be in a hurry to move. At first you will feel very uncomfortable on the ice, as though your feet want to run away with you and your ankles are weak. Bend your knees more and try pushing or gliding along on each skate. Keep the steps small. On no account walk.

Once you have got used to the ice, then is the time to attempt the four basic techniques which are moving forwards, backwards, stopping and starting.

Moving and stopping

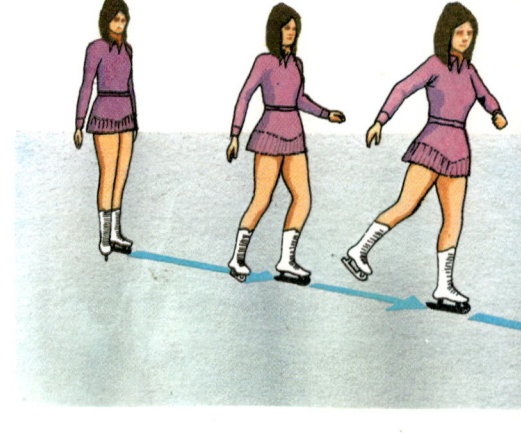

Once you have mastered these basic techniques you can enjoy skating without going any further. After a while you will want to go on to the more advanced techniques.

▼ If you know the very basics you can have a lot of fun at the ice rink. Those who are not quite ready for the ice can watch from the sidelines.

▲ **Starting position**
Put your right foot behind your left, so that the instep of the right foot is against the heel of the left, forming a "T".

Skating forwards

Transfer the weight on to the left foot and move forwards on the left foot. Make sure you push forward on the whole length of the blade's inside edge and never on the toe. As you glide forward keep your left leg bent and your right leg extended behind you as far as it will reach. Keep your right foot just clear of the ice and bring it up beside the left one. Now repeat the action turning out the left foot and pushing on to the right foot. Transfer the weight on to it. Look ahead and bring the opposite shoulder to foot forward as in walking.

Stopping

To perform the "T" stop, place the instep of the right foot against the heel of the left foot. Make sure the blade is off the ice. Slowly lower the right foot until the outside edge touches the ice. Touch lightly at first then apply pressure.

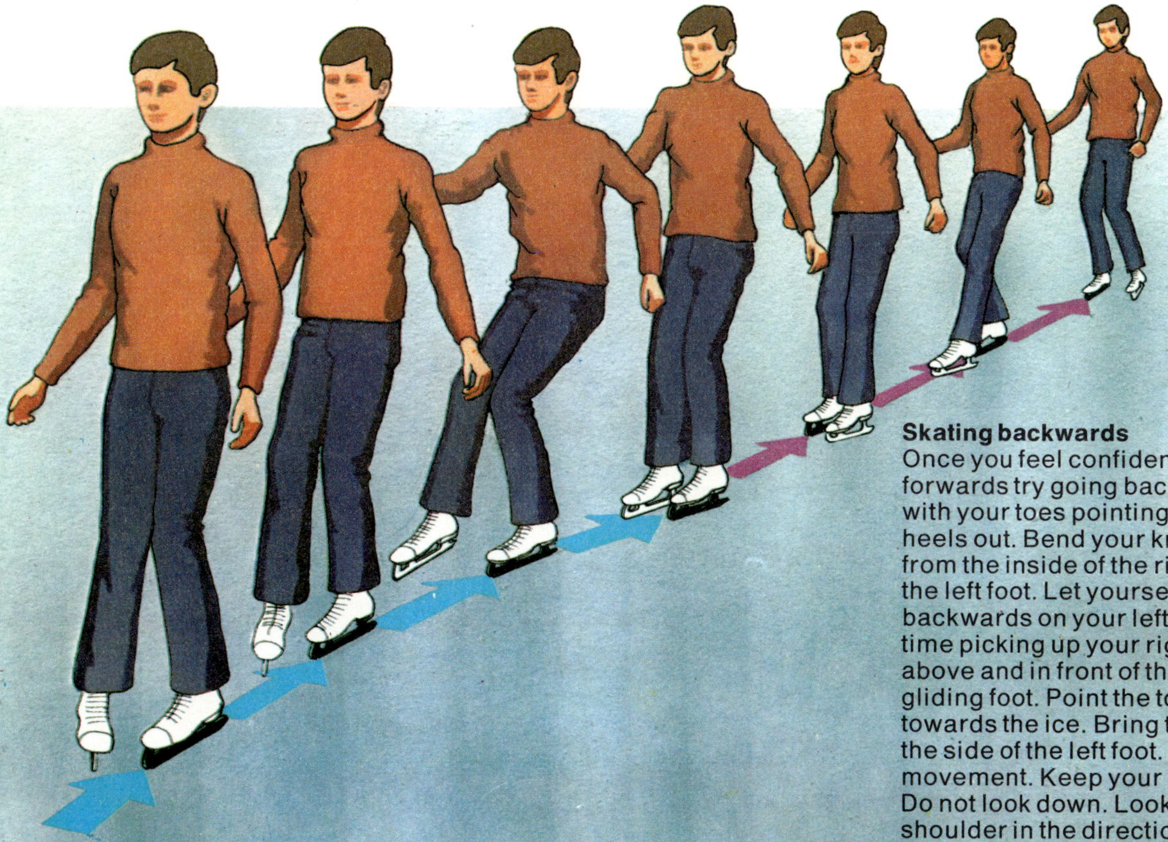

Skating backwards

Once you feel confident at skating forwards try going backwards. Stand with your toes pointing in and your heels out. Bend your knees and push from the inside of the right blade on to the left foot. Let yourself glide backwards on your left foot at the same time picking up your right foot, just above and in front of the toe of the gliding foot. Point the toe down towards the ice. Bring the free leg to the side of the left foot. Repeat the movement. Keep your body upright. Do not look down. Look over your shoulder in the direction you want to go.

Figures and jumps

There are more than 50 figures that can be performed in figure skating. The compulsory figures for championships are chosen by a lottery system each year. These must be performed as accurately and fluently as possible.

In free skating skaters present a programme to include spins and jumps that suit their style best. This must be done within a time limit. Skaters may choose their own music. In figure-skating championships contestants have to be good at both figure and free skating. Marks are awarded for each section and added together for the final total.

Ice dancing is like ballroom dancing on ice and includes dances such as the waltz, quickstep and tango. The couple can skate side by side, facing each other or one behind the other but they must not break away for more than a few seconds in order to change positions. In competitions there are two sections, one compulsory and the other free.

Pair skating is a combination of dancing and free skating. The most impressive feature is the lift when the man lifts his partner above his head. The skaters have free choice of programme and music. Not all their movements have to be identical but they must move in harmony.

Speed skating is very different from figure skating. Ice racers use special long blades which allow them to average 45 kph (28mph). There are two sizes of oval track. On the shorter track there are three types of races: individual, relay and the gruelling pursuit between two competing skaters.

Skating for champions

Once you have mastered the basic techniques you may wish to concentrate on one of the various types of skating. There are plenty to choose from: ice hockey, speed skating or the intricate arabesques of figure skating. When you have learnt some of the basic figures add some elementary spirals, jumps and linking steps. Now you will be able to make up a short free-skating programme.

Outside forward eight
The diagram shows one version of a figure eight. Starting on the right-forward-outside edge trace a perfect circle, changing feet at the intersection and ending the figure where you started. To perform this figure well you must start correctly.

The abbreviations show the foot, direction of movement and edge of blade used in a figure.
rfo: right forwards outside
lfo: left forwards outside
lbo: left backwards outside
Tbi: Threes backwards inside

Threes to centre
This movement turns you from forward to backward on one foot drawing a figure 3 on the ice with the blade. The complete figure makes two 3s facing each other. The forward outside 3 is used most out of all the turns. The circles should be of equal size.

Backward change of edge
This is a three-circle figure. All the circles should be the same size. The mistakes here can be caused by lack of speed, faulty positioning of weight, arms and head, or wrong use of edges. The

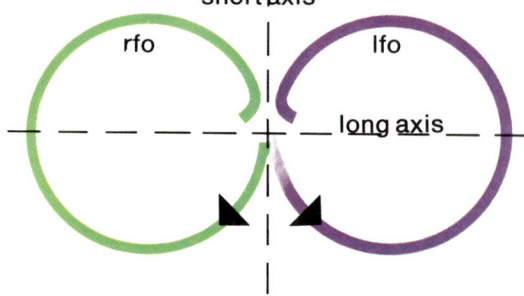

green line: right foot
mauve line: left foot
dotted line: common faults in skating figures

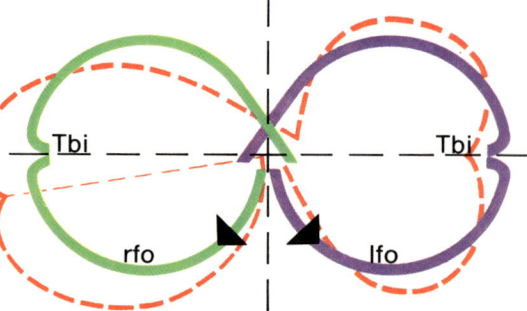

figure involves making a half circle then a change of edge, a full circle, followed by another half circle another change of edge and then a complete circle to finish.

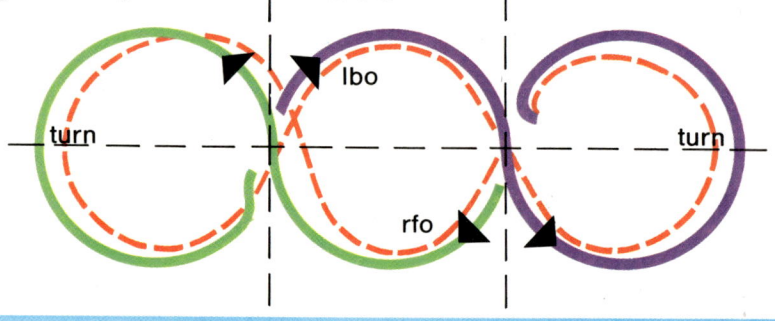

Compulsory figures

In major championships three compulsory figures are required which must be skated three times on each foot. Judges give marks for each figure. They take into account the shape of the figure, how gracefully it is executed, the carriage of the skater, the exactness of the footwork and the speed.

▼ The natural poise and perfect timing of ice dancing. Harmony with both the music and your partner is essential.

Pairs and free skating

Each judge awards two marks for each performance. One is for technical merit and the other for artistic impression. This means that not only are the contents of the programme important but also the choice of music and general harmony. The scale of marks runs from one to six to one decimal point. Together the judges display the marks they have awarded by holding up large cards with the number shown.

Jumps

Out of more than thirty internationally accepted jumps there are a few which have become famous because of their difficulty and beauty. The success of the jump depends very much on the strength of the spring and also on the timing. You must think first of going up, then of turning, and then of making a sure and steady landing.

Axel Paulsen jump

Named after its originator, this breathtaking jump is probably the most famous of all. It involves making one and a half turns in the air. It is a combination of a "three jump" and a "loop jump".

Double Lutz jump

The Lutz jump is one of the most difficult to perform. It involves turning in an anti-clockwise direction. The landing from this jump is on the opposite foot to that used in the take-off.

Double one-foot Salchow jump

It is name after the Swedish skater Ulrich Salchow. The single jump is from the inside back making a loop in the air and landing on the outside back of the other foot. The double version makes two revolutions.

The ice rink

One of the first mechanically refrigerated ice rinks was built in London in 1876 using ether as a coolant. It had a surface of 12 m × 7.5 m (40 × 24 ft). Before this was opened the Scandinavians and Canadians had a great advantage in skating with their long frozen winters. Other countries did not have such long winters. They had to wait years for a severe frost to freeze their lakes sufficiently for skating. In the 1930s many artificial rinks were made and they became major centres of entertainment with the growth of ice pantomimes. Many large towns now have public ice rinks where anyone can skate.

Some fine indoor rinks have been built. They are run by trained staff including managers, instructors and engineers. The engineers maintain the ice-making plant and keep the surface in the right condition for skating on. Championships require extra careful planning and organization from the staff.

There is considerably more to an ice rink than a surface to skate on. For the skaters there are changing rooms, skate-fitting and sharpening services, a shop selling equipment, a bar, a restaurant, and medical services. There is also adequate seating in a warmed area for spectators.

Music is an important part of skating not only for the professional but for providing a social atmosphere for general skating. The old-fashioned Hammond organs are less common now. They have been replaced by electronic organs and stereo music from cassettes.

Making thin ice

An ice rink can be anything from the small open-air village rink to the specially designed indoor rink with a standard international size of 60m × 30m (195 × 98ft). These rinks have large freezing units and good ice preparation services with facilities for skaters and spectators.

Advertising
In many ice rinks colourful advertising is carried on the safety barriers in panels and space is rented. Good coverage is ensured if the ice rink is used for television.

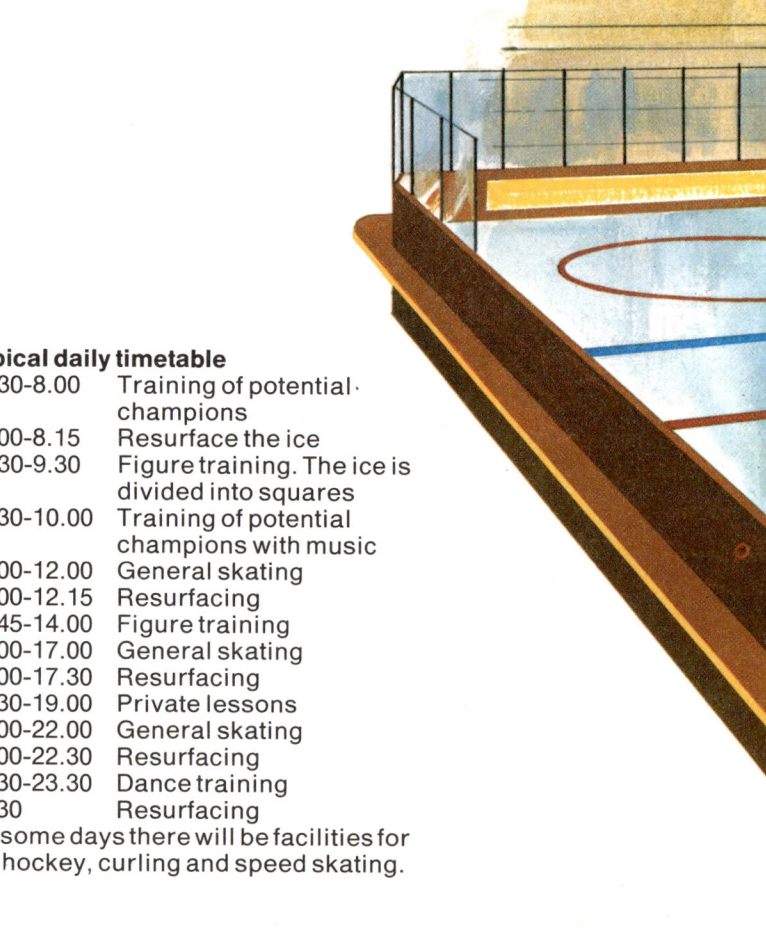

Typical daily timetable
5.30-8.00	Training of potential champions
8.00-8.15	Resurface the ice
8.30-9.30	Figure training. The ice is divided into squares
9.30-10.00	Training of potential champions with music
10.00-12.00	General skating
12.00-12.15	Resurfacing
12.45-14.00	Figure training
14.00-17.00	General skating
17.00-17.30	Resurfacing
17.30-19.00	Private lessons
19.00-22.00	General skating
22.00-22.30	Resurfacing
22.30-23.30	Dance training
23.30	Resurfacing

On some days there will be facilities for ice hockey, curling and speed skating.

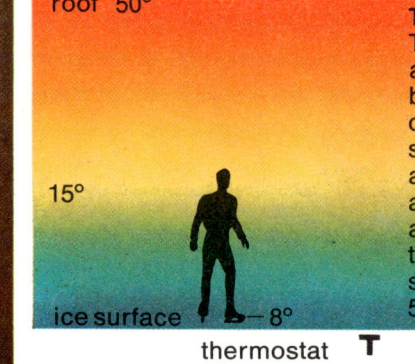

roof 50°

15°

ice surface −8°

thermostat **T**   water sensor

Temperature
The ice surface has a temperature of about −8°C (18°F) which is maintained by thermostats set into the ice and connected to the freezing plant. Water sensors on the ice surface register the amount of water formed. At 1.5m (5ft) above the ice, the temperature is held at about 15°C (60°F) for the comfort of the skaters. Roof lights can raise the surrounding air to a temperature of 50°C (120°F).

Outside rinks

► Open-air rinks can vary from the small mountain-village ice rink to the large rink in a town with all facilities. Small rinks are often made by banking snow into the shape of a rink then flooding the area and allowing it to freeze naturally. In many cases there are no safety barriers, making it difficult for beginners. The larger outdoor rinks may be built to professional standards with freezing pipes and plant and everything but a roof.

advertising

Surfacing

After use, the surface of the ice becomes rough and difficult to skate on and must be resurfaced. A machine cuts the ice and sucks up the scraping as it moves forwards. At the same time water is sprayed from the back of the machine onto the ice and freezes to form a new surface.

resurfacing machine

ice

freezing pipes

concrete

warm air pad

concrete base

Freezing Plant

This is usually at one end of the ice rink and one level below the rink surface. It is built into a sound-proofed room. A typical plant has two compressors, one acting as a standby which can also be cut in when extra freezing is required. The operation is automatic. The coolant in the tubes may be an ammonia-brine solution.

Floor

This is a solid concrete base over which a warm air pad is formed. This pad stops frost from the freezing tubes passing through the base into the surrounding earth and forming a frost layer. A layer of concrete or sand is placed over the warm air pad into which are set cast-iron freezing tubes. Further concrete or sand is placed over the freezing pipes and then the surface flooded with water to a depth of 5cm (2 in).

Ice hockey

This tough, hard-tackling game was probably first played on Kingston Harbour, Ontario in 1860. Rules and regulations were devised in 1879 by W. F. Robertson, a student from McGill University and a keen skater. The first team formed was the McGill University Hockey Club with the new team size of nine players a side. In 1893 teams began to compete for the Stanley Cup, the main trophy in ice hockey. At the beginning of this century the sport began to grow in Europe. The French took up the game in 1908 and it was a Frenchman, Louis Magnus, who was responsible for the formation of the International Ice Hockey Federation.

For a long time the powerful Canadians dominated the international play but their supremacy was challenged when they were beaten by the Russians in 1956. Since then Eastern European countries have been fielding strong teams.

The game consists of three periods of 25 minutes each. There are two referees and six players from each team are allowed on at one time. Each team usually has about twelve players in all. Reserves are regularly being brought on if only to confuse the opponents. The amount of protective clothing is an indication of the battling and fierce nature of the game.

Bandy, still played in Sweden, is another form of ice hockey. It is played on a larger rink with a ball instead of a puck and there are eleven players in a team. Unlike ice hockey, no play is allowed behind the goal.

Hard and fast

Ice hockey is a combination of skating skills, tactics and speed which make it one of the most exciting of team games. The bullet-like puck and flailing hockey sticks are some reasons for the players wearing their thick protective padding.

The protective helmet is usually made of nylon. For senior players it is optional, but juniors must wear one. The goalkeeper also wears a face mask.

Brightly-coloured team shirts are worn over the protective clothing.

Boots and skates
Ice-hockey boots have a low ankle support, reinforced toes and well-padded tongues. The skate blade is narrow with a plain, pointed front end.

All players wear padding on their shoulders and elbows.

A thick padded shield and glove are worn by the goalkeeper to protect him from high shots.

The lower part of the goalkeeper's stick is slightly wider than that of the other players'.

Goalkeeper

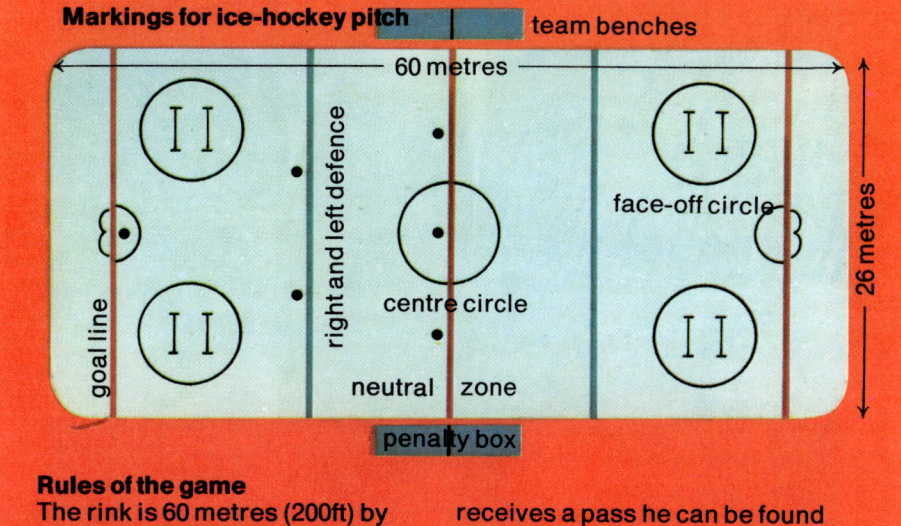

Markings for ice-hockey pitch   team benches

60 metres

right and left defence

face-off circle

26 metres

goal line

centre circle

neutral   zone

penalty box

Face off
Play at the beginning of each period and after a goal begins with face off. The puck is dropped by the referee in the centre of the rink between the sticks of the two centre forwards. Face offs start the game again after a foul.

Rules of the game
The rink is 60 metres (200ft) by 26 metres (85ft) and the game is played with a puck made of vulcanized rubber and wooden sticks. A player may stop the puck with his hand, body or skate. He may kick the puck but may not score from a kick. If a player is wrongly positioned when he receives a pass he can be found offside.

By the side of the rink there is a penalty box, sometimes called the "sin bin". Players are sent there for fouling, for one, two or more minutes. A substitute player may not take the place of a player in the penalty box.

Fouls
Ice hockey does not enjoy the reputation of being the world's friendliest game. The referees have a full-time job looking out for fouls. You must not hook another player with the stick, elbow, hold or deliberately skate into him. You must not use your stick to poke him with the small end, spear him with the wide end or trip him up. If a player throws something on to the ice rink from the bench he will be heavily penalized, but there will only be a minor penalty if he deliberately moves the goal. The referee will stop play if a spectator throws an object on to the ice or physically hampers a player. A face off is called for if the puck disappears from the referee's view. It has been known for a second puck to appear on the ice. This is illegal.

▶ A violent clash of sticks and bodies in this international match between Sweden and Czechoslovakia played at Sapporo in 1972.

Excitement and drama

Skating shown on television makes excellent entertainment, from the excitement of World Competitions to the spectacle of a big ice show. Many of the classical pantomimes, like Cinderella, have been presented as lavish ice shows with a very large cast. The lead is usually taken by an ex-championship skater who has turned professional. The cast are skaters who perform all the movements and action, the words and songs are relayed over hidden loudspeakers by people watching the skaters making sure the words match the action.

Ice and snow have often provided a background for thrillers. There are the situations where a group of people are cut off by snow; exciting chases over mountain slopes and glaciers by expert skiers; tense moments when people are walking across a frozen lake and the ice begins to crack; or someone hurtling down a bobsleigh track to possible death. Ice and snow make beautiful, but menacing, scenery which adds to their attraction in books, films and plays.

In *Cinerama Holiday* the camera was mounted on the front of a bobsleigh so you felt as if you were bobsleighing down the track too. Heroes perched precariously on top of cable cars is another film stunt that is particularly nerve wracking. Very often local ski instructors and residents are used as "stand ins" in these films for the stunts, as they are among the best skiers there are. Whether you have been winter sporting or not, snow and ice certainly add to the excitement of entertainment and drama.

Some spectacular moments

Snow or ice is the main background for all these films and the pantomime. Pantomimes on ice have been popular for many years, all the actors have to be good at both skating and acting. Filming in the mountains is an extremely complicated affair. One of the main difficulties is placing the cameras so that the skiing looks as dramatic as possible.

▶ The start of the dramatic snowmobile race in the film *Snowball Express*.

▼ Sonja Henie was the star of many skating films in the 1930s. Nowadays her technical ability would not be considered very great, but she won many prizes and Olympic medals then.

▲ In the film *Ski Raiders* ex-Olympic champion, Jean-Claude Killy played a bank robber. He robbed a bank in the Italian alps and hid the money in a perilous glacier. In this scene he is skiing down the glacier.

►*Downhill Racer* was a film starring the actor Robert Redford, who is an extremely good skier. The film examines the life of a professional skier and shows the main difficulties and pressures that professional skiers face.

▼Cinderella has always been a favourite subject for pantomimes. Here it is given a spectacular treatment on ice.

Curling

Curling is similar to bowls, but played on ice, although curlers prefer to say that bowls is similar to curling but it is played on grass. A player sends a large granite stone across the ice trying to get as near the centre of the marked rings, or "house", as is possible. This point is called the "tee" in Europe and "button" in North America. There are two teams, or rinks, each with four players. The four are called the lead, second, third and skip. Each player delivers two stones, sixteen stones completing an "end", or "head". There are ten or twelve ends in a game.

The curler stands on the hack, or starting point, and swings the stone backwards and follows it through, giving the stone a twist so that it rotates to left or right before it reaches the tee. As the stone slides along the ice two other members of the team move even faster than the stone sweeping furiously to clear the stone's path. Curling involves a lot of skill and it is surprisingly energetic.

Sweeping is an extremely important part of curling. Curlers sweep the stone before they deliver it to make sure that there is no ice stuck to it which might make it slide more slowly. As a stone reaches the circle the team may sweep even more vigorously to persuade the stone to slide another centimetre or two. Curlers have to be very agile to sweep as the stone travels down the rink as their brooms must never touch the stone. As you can see in the pictures European and North American curlers use slightly different brooms.

Sweeping and sliding

Curling originated in Scotland at least 400 years ago. It is now included in the Winter Olympics. Modern curling is a game of skill rather than strength. It is becoming a more and more popular sport, played on indoor rinks as well as outdoors. In Canada, for example, there are more curlers than golfers.

▼ Competitions between clubs are called "bonspiels". The beautiful Scottish countryside makes this bonspiel particularly colourful.

The skip is the leader of the curling team. He stands behind the house directing his team with shouts and gestures. He tells each player where to aim and whether he should try to hit another stone. As soon as the stone is sliding down the rink the other two members run along in front of it until the skip gives the order to sweep the ice in front of the stone.

4.25 metres

◄ The oldest known curling stone is called the Stirling Stone. It has the date 1511 carved on it. The heaviest stone found weighs 53kg (117lb). Curling stones used today must not weigh more than 20kg (44lb). They should be 30cm (1ft) in circumference and 10-12cm (4-5in) high. The stone is concave on the top and underneath so that only the rim of the stone touches the ice.

  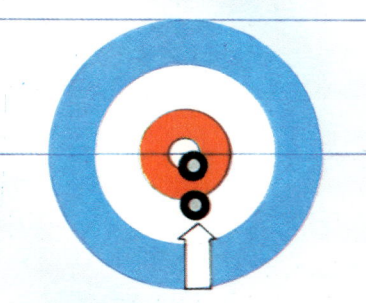

Wick and roll
This is when one stone pushes a rival stone out of the way. At the end of the head each stone nearer the tee than an opposing stone scores a point. This move can be vital.

Freeze
A stone that stops just in front of an opponent's stone is called a freeze. If the next throw hits the covering stone it may also move the other stone as well.

Guard
Guard really explains itself. One stone is positioned to guard another stone from being knocked out. Sometimes there are several stones in the house in this position.

▲ The concentration of these curlers emphasizes the importance of sweeping. After a stone has been delivered, two curlers from the playing team can sweep the path in front of the stone from the nearest hog score to the sweeping score. The skip tells them when to start sweeping. Once the stone is beyond the sweeping score either skip can sweep round it.

The rink, or sheet as it is sometimes called, is 42 metres (46yds) long and 4.25 metres (14ft) wide. The starting point, or hack, is a metal-covered foothold on the foot-score line. No part of the curler's body or equipment must pass the nearest hog score during delivery.

Before the curler delivers the stone he will brush it thoroughly, to free it of ice. Starting with one foot on the back the curler slides forwards with one leg bent and the other leg trailing behind and releases the stone.

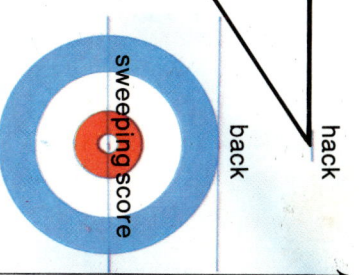

hog score

sweeping score

back

hack

42 metres

◄ High up on the ice wall, a four-man bob team rushes round a bend.

► The Japanese two-man bob speeds down the ice-packed course.

NIPPON
II

Bobsleighs   *The shortest way down*

Sledges for speed

To many people, even those who have tobogganed down fairly steep slopes, bobsleighing looks frighteningly fast and dangerous. Teams of two or four people ride a bobsleigh down a specially made track as fast as they possibly can. This can mean travelling at over 120 kph (75 mph) on the straight.

The bobsleigh track has a base of stone on concrete, on top of which wet snow and water have frozen to form a solid surface. The course is at least 1500 metres (1 mile) long and is made up of curves and bends as well as straight sections. The bobs reach such a speed that they can go round the corners on the wall of the course rather than on the ground. The walls of the curves are up to 6 metres (18 ft) high and are usually concave. Even the straight sections have tall walls so that the bobs do not go off the course.

The start of a bobsleigh race is especially exciting. The whole team pushes the bob to get it moving. When the bob starts to gather speed the team jumps on. The race can start with a "flying start" or a "standing start". For a flying start the team starts to push the bob from 15 metres (15 yds) behind the start line and is timed from the moment the front runners cross the start line. For a standing start the bob is pushed from the start line and is timed from there.

As the bob goes round a corner the team must be certain that they are leaning in the right direction. One false move by one member could upset the bob, with disastrous results.

Courses they take

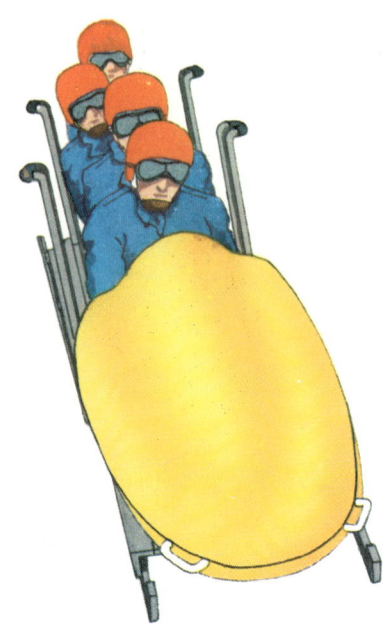

There are bobsleigh runs all over the world. One of the most famous lies parallel to the Cresta run in St Moritz, Switzerland. The two tracks are similar, the Cresta run being slightly steeper, and therefore faster, than the bob run. The bobsleigh run is for teams of two or four people, the Cresta run is braved by just one person at a time. Both these runs are specially built for the winter season. The curves and bends in the Cresta are all named, each one having its own history of drama and disaster.

◄ A bobsleigh has two front runners and two back runners. The front runners are attached to a front axle and steer the bob, rear runners are attached to a rear axle. The front man steers the bob with rope or a wheel connected to the front axle. Between the runners there is a brake. This is only used in emergencies as its edges can damage the run and make it dangerous for other bobs.

▼ As with a four-man bob, the front man in a two-man bob steers and the back man operates the brake. The handles on the side and back of the bob are for pushing off at the start. The design of bobsleighs has changed over the years so that they are now about as streamlined as they could possibly be.

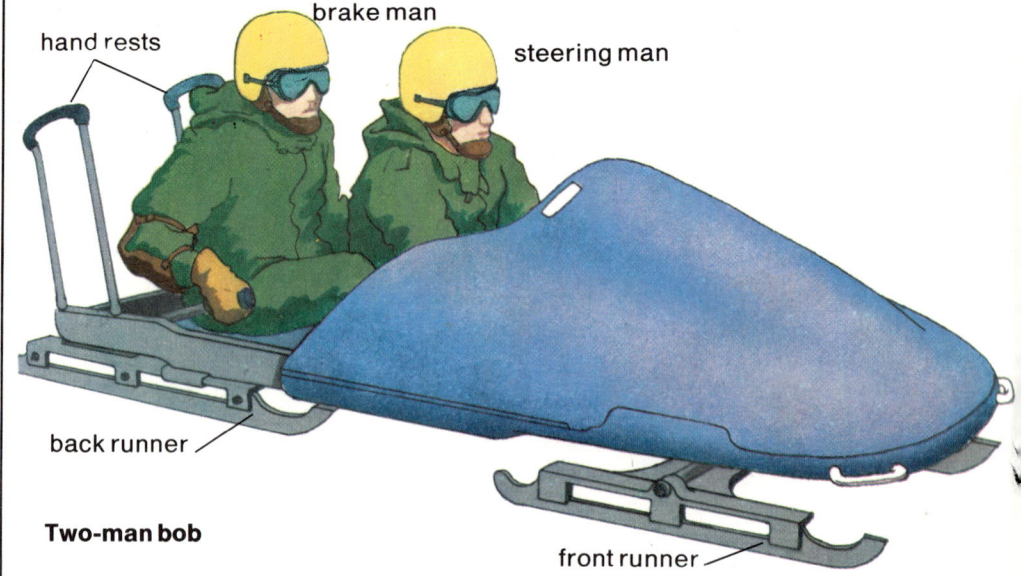

hand rests

brake man

steering man

back runner

Two-man bob

front runner

The Cresta skeleton

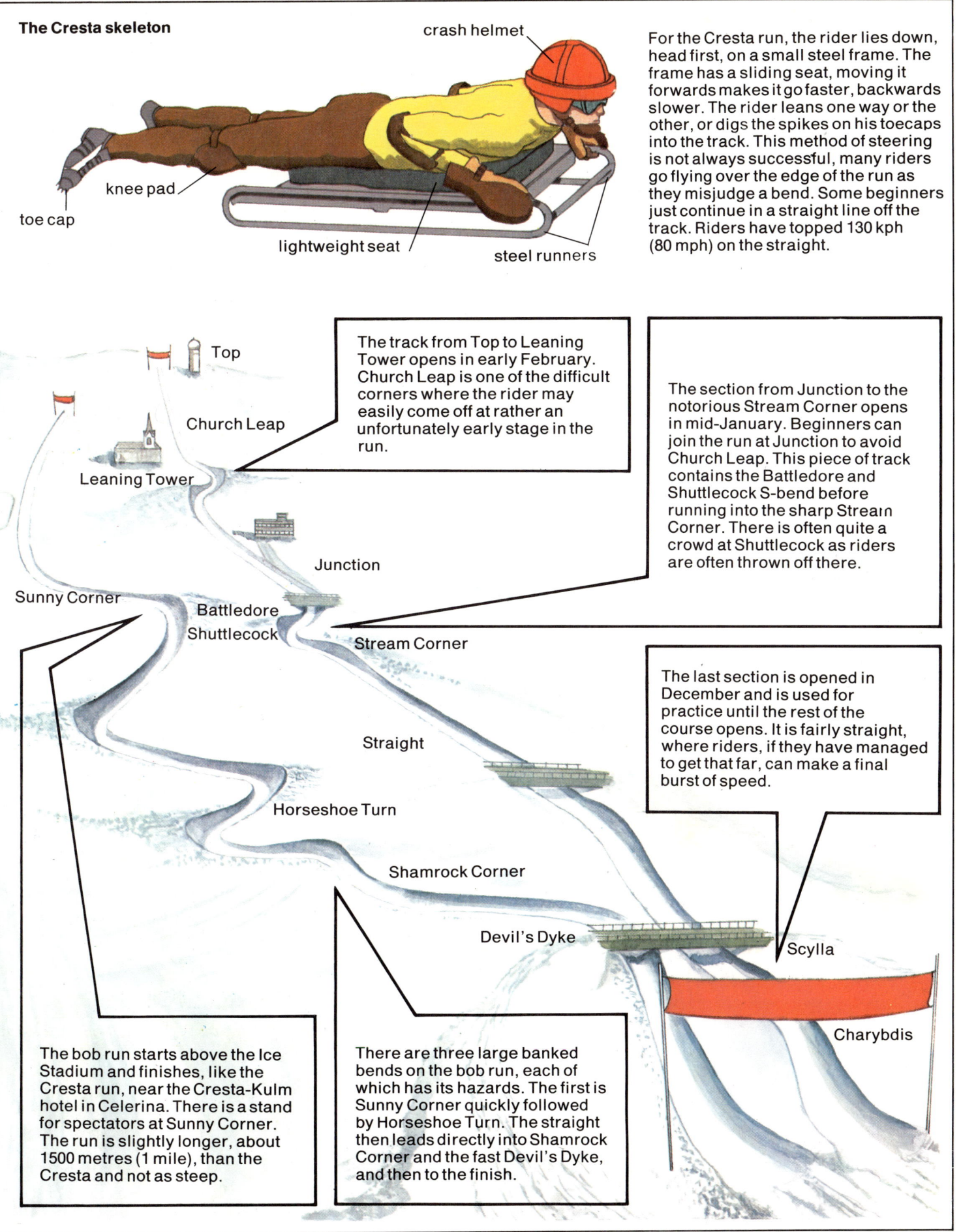

crash helmet

knee pad

toe cap

lightweight seat

steel runners

For the Cresta run, the rider lies down, head first, on a small steel frame. The frame has a sliding seat, moving it forwards makes it go faster, backwards slower. The rider leans one way or the other, or digs the spikes on his toecaps into the track. This method of steering is not always successful, many riders go flying over the edge of the run as they misjudge a bend. Some beginners just continue in a straight line off the track. Riders have topped 130 kph (80 mph) on the straight.

Top

Church Leap

Leaning Tower

Sunny Corner

Junction

Battledore
Shuttlecock

Stream Corner

Straight

Horseshoe Turn

Shamrock Corner

Devil's Dyke

Scylla

Charybdis

The track from Top to Leaning Tower opens in early February. Church Leap is one of the difficult corners where the rider may easily come off at rather an unfortunately early stage in the run.

The section from Junction to the notorious Stream Corner opens in mid-January. Beginners can join the run at Junction to avoid Church Leap. This piece of track contains the Battledore and Shuttlecock S-bend before running into the sharp Stream Corner. There is often quite a crowd at Shuttlecock as riders are often thrown off there.

The last section is opened in December and is used for practice until the rest of the course opens. It is fairly straight, where riders, if they have managed to get that far, can make a final burst of speed.

The bob run starts above the Ice Stadium and finishes, like the Cresta run, near the Cresta-Kulm hotel in Celerina. There is a stand for spectators at Sunny Corner. The run is slightly longer, about 1500 metres (1 mile), than the Cresta and not as steep.

There are three large banked bends on the bob run, each of which has its hazards. The first is Sunny Corner quickly followed by Horseshoe Turn. The straight then leads directly into Shamrock Corner and the fast Devil's Dyke, and then to the finish.

Toboggans

Tobogganing ranges from the tin tray you slide down a hill at home on, to the very carefully designed luge which speeds down a specially made course.

For practical purposes toboggans are still used by some people living in mountain villages. Mothers put their babies in a pram fixed on to the toboggan and elderly people use them to go from one village to another carrying milk or other necessities. At night you may see the pretty sight of a stream of light from people's toboggans as they travel down the mountain.

One of the most popular toboggans is the Davos toboggan, named after a village in Switzerland. It is made of wood with metal runners. Some toboggans have quite complicated steering and braking systems, but most people steer with a piece of rope and brake with their feet, if they are going down feet first. It is better not to go head first down a hill that is too steep unless you are sure that you will be able to stop easily.

Sledges are large toboggans. Eskimos still use sledges drawn by husky dogs for transporting goods over the ice and snow. Eskimo sledges used to be made from whale bone. They covered the pieces they wanted joined together with water, until it froze solid. Horse-drawn sledges were also popular in countries with a great deal of ice and snow in the winter, like the Soviet Union where these sledges were called troikas. Today horse-drawn sledges are still used for visitors to mountain villages in Austria and Switzerland.

Exhilarating at any level

The differences between tobogganing and lugeing are not very great. The main ones are speed and surface. Lugeing is a very fast sport, tobogganing can be as slow as you like ; lugers race on a specially made course, but you can toboggan on any hill with only a little snow.

Lugeing
Lugeing is one of the newest Olympic sports. The competitor speeds down a course of bends and curves, lying on his back only a few centimetres off the ground, on a toboggan without any brakes. From the waist upwards the luger's body is off the toboggan. The further you lean back the faster you go. The competitor steers by leaning in one direction or another, or by pulling the strap attached to the front runners. To go around the curves you use your shoulders to steer the toboggan right on to the wall of the curve, and then use the weight of your whole body and legs to come out of the curve back on to the straight. In competitions each luger has four runs, the person with the fastest average time is the winner.

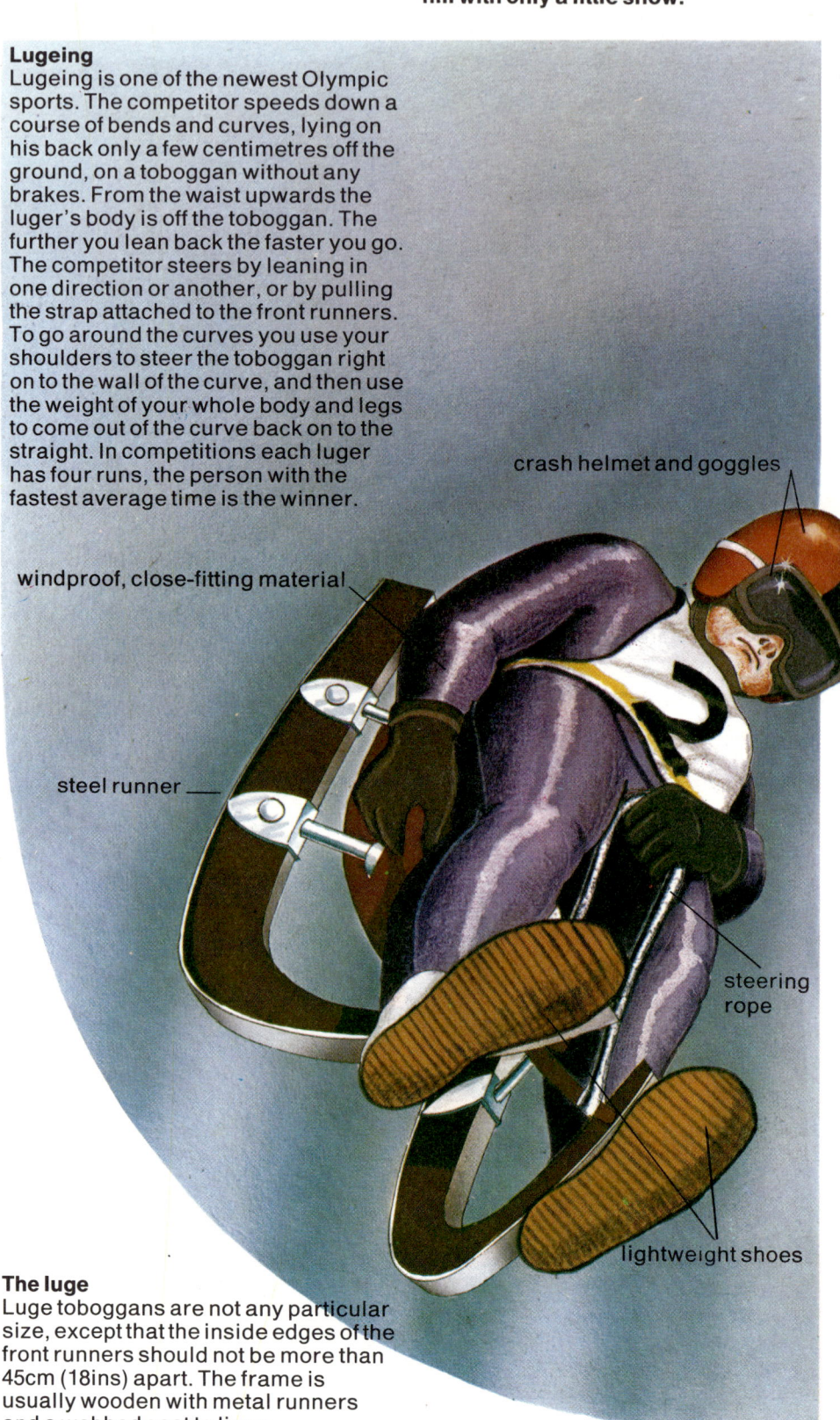

crash helmet and goggles

windproof, close-fitting material

steel runner

steering rope

lightweight shoes

The luge
Luge toboggans are not any particular size, except that the inside edges of the front runners should not be more than 45cm (18ins) apart. The frame is usually wooden with metal runners and a webbed seat to lie on.

▲ Steering wheels on toboggans are either attached to the seat, which will move the body weight and therefore the toboggan, or they are attached to runners.

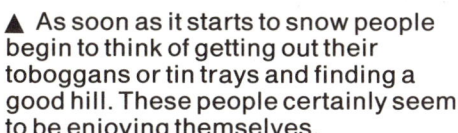
▲ As soon as it starts to snow people begin to think of getting out their toboggans or tin trays and finding a good hill. These people certainly seem to be enjoying themselves.

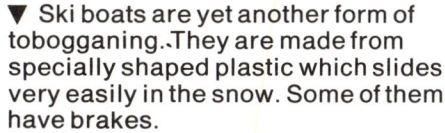
▼ Ski boats are yet another form of tobogganing. They are made from specially shaped plastic which slides very easily in the snow. Some of them have brakes.

Races between dog-pulled sledges are very popular in North America. There are always at least seven husky dogs in a team. The driver stands on the back of the sledge and controls and directs the team from there with the harness and a whip. These races sometimes last several days.

Mountains in winter

One of the most important and enjoyable aspects of winter sports is the scenery and the countryside. Most winter sports resorts are attractive villages set in beautiful mountainous or hilly surroundings. In the mountains the sky is much bluer than at lower levels, which makes the contrast between the sky and the snow particularly striking. In the early morning you can go out after a fall of snow during the night to the marvellously still and peaceful sight of the mountains covered with untouched snow.

Going to a skiing resort does not necessarily mean that you have to ski all the time. For the adventurous there is mountaineering which should always be done with a qualified guide. The less energetic can spend their time gaining a healthy sun tan. It can also be a pleasure to simply observe the traditional way of life in mountain villages.

Most resorts have a wide variety of activities, some to be enjoyed during the day, others in the evening. Après ski, which is French for after ski, is the general name for the evening's entertainment. The variety of amusements depends on the size of the resort, but in every resort there will be a bar and cafe where you can drink glühwein and a restaurant where you can eat fondue. Most places also have somewhere you can dance to a juke box, disco or a local group.

Although it is usually very cold when the sun has set there is often floodlight skating, torchlight skiing and tobogganing and horse-drawn sleigh rides through the snow.

The numerous possibilities

When they have finished their outdoor sports, whatever it might be, most people gather in the cafes to have a warm drink and some cakes. After they have changed out of their thick outdoor clothes they then have dinner. After dinner is the time for dancing, drinking, and talking in bars and cafes.

▼ The sun setting behind the mountains is one of the most lovely of all the beautiful sights you will see. Clouds sometimes gather in the evenings if there is to be a fall of snow during the night.

◄ Curling is one of the sports you can take part in at a winter resort. This type of curling is very similar to bowls. The thrower tries to hit a small wooden block at the other end of the rink with a type of curling stone.

▲ To eat a cheese fondue you dip a stick with bread on the end into a central dish of cheese, which is kept warm over a small flame. There are also meat fondues where you dip pieces of meat into a central dish of hot oil.

Geneva Fondue
A traditional après-ski dish you can try at home. The fondue cooks over a heater on the table and you dip in your bread on sticks.
8 egg yolks
250g Gruyère cheese
150g butter
$\frac{1}{3}$ litre cream
Fried bread
Pepper, salt, grated nutmeg to season.
Mix egg yolks, cheese, pepper, nutmeg and salt in saucepan over gentle heat without boiling. Add butter, bit by bit, still stirring. When mixture thickens add cream.

Glühwein
A warming drink after an exhausting day's skiing. You can make this just as well with cider. For four large mugs you will need:
2 slices lemon
2 whole cloves
2 tablespoons caster sugar
$1\frac{1}{2}$ sticks cinnamon
$\frac{1}{2}$ litre red wine
Stick the cloves into the lemon slices. Put the lemon, sugar and cinnamon into a saucepan and stir until the sugar has melted. Pour in the red wine. Just before it boils take it off the heat. Take out lemon and cinnamon and pour into mugs.

A career in skating

You have to be exceptionally good to become a champion or a star in any winter sport. Many hours of training on ski slopes or ice rinks must come first and this needs dedication. It can also be expensive.

The younger you begin the better. It is often said that children living in snowy areas can ski before they can walk. In skiing it is best to start off by joining one of the junior clubs such as the junior section of the Kandahar Club. Your progress will be observed and if you do well you will be entered by your club for the National Junior Ski Championship and then possibly chosen by the National Ski Federation for the Olympic team.

If you want to represent your country in skating you will have to pass a series of tests before you can go on for professional training. Then if you do very well you will be entered for the Bronze, Silver and Gold certificates. Your national skating association might then select you for European and world championships.

The competitive figure skater must remain an amateur but ice shows and pantomimes have professional casts from the animated trees to the glittering ice maidens. This show business world is not easy to get into and is very demanding if you do. (In some countries you are fined for falling over in a performance.)

In North America ice hockey has a similar status to soccer in Europe. There are both amateur and professional leagues. With the formation of the London Lions in 1973, ice hockey has been given a great boost in Britain.

Skating to stardom

Ice skating at championship level is challenging and demanding. It requires many hours of practice, courage and determination. Judy was going to need all these to get to the top.

Judy was skilful on roller skates before she started ice skating.

At a rehearsal Pat, who was in the lead part, fell and broke her ankle.

On the night of the pantomime Doug Day was there, the famous trainer. He was very impressed with Judy's performance.

6 O'CLOCK ST MORNING, J BED

Doug Day took on Judy as a pupil. He made her work hard. She had to do compulsory figures, spins and jumps.

Snowmobiles

The snowmobile is a motorized sledge. It has two steering runners at the front and it is driven by a single caterpillar-track which lies along the middle and at the back. The track is powered by a petrol engine at the front of the machine. The driver and passengers sit astride a padded seat just behind the engine. At the back of the seat there is a combined back-rest and storage box.

The first models of snowmobiles were made at the beginning of this century, but it has only been over the last ten years that snowmobiling has really caught on. Trappers and hunters often use them in preference to dog teams, Eskimos in Canada use them, but they are more commonly used for fun than as a means of transport.

In Canada snow "safaris" are popular. Families follow cross-country trails on large three-seater models or with the smaller "ski-doos" which can easily be handled by children.

Specially designed snowmobiles are used for racing. Some models can go over 160 kph (100 mph). Snowmobile racing is an exciting and spectacular event. The rider jams open the throttle at the start of the race and as the track bites into the snow the front of the machine rises into the air. Expert riders use their body weight to gain advantage on the bends. Some races are run on oval tracks such as the "1500" at Sault Ste Marie, Michigan, whereas the Midnight Sun 600 in Alaska is a cross-country race lasting three days covering over 966 km (600 miles).

In 1922 Joseph-Armand Bombardier built this snowmobile at the age of 15. It had a large propellor blade at the rear. Bombardier developed and built snowmobiles which led to the modern ski-doo.

Many people now explore the snow-bound regions of North America in winter. One of the biggest hazards is running out of petrol.

Glossary

Anorak Wind, shower and snowproof jacket, with zipped front and pockets, usually having a hood.

Avalanche stop Wooden barrier erected to prevent the formation of avalanches. It may naturally occur in the form of trees.

Basket Circular section placed near the end of a ski stick to prevent the stick sinking in the snow.

Bindings Device for attaching the ski to the boot.

Bloodwagon Stretcher, sometimes with runners, used for carrying injured skiers.

Bonspiel Curling competition involving many teams.

Cable car Rectangular cabin hanging under and running on a cable used for mountain transport. Can carry up to 100 people.

Camel spin Spin in figure skating. This is done with one leg stretched out horizontally and the other remains upright.

Carriage Position of a skater's body while doing figure skating. Judges will award marks for a graceful and relaxed carriage.

Chairlift Single or double seat suspended from a cable used for taking people to ski slopes.

Christiania Method of turning and stopping named after the town of Christiania—the original name for Oslo, the capital city of Norway.

Cleat Protruding section of the caterpillar track which drives a snowmobile. The cleat digs into the snow and provides traction.

Cresta Hamlet near St Moritz, Switzerland. Gives its name to the Cresta Run—a scientifically constructed track for specially-made one man skeletons.

Directional flags Used in downhill and slalom courses, red flags are placed down the left side, and green down the right.

Drag lift Ski lift used to tow a skier up the mountain by a moving cable.

Edges Sides of the ski which must be sharpened and are used, when angled, to grip the snow when making turns. Also the sides of a skating blade.

FIS Fédération Internationale de Ski. First ski organization founded in France in 1924. Its function is to organize and control ski competitions.

Fondue Originally a Swiss cheese dish eaten by dipping bread into seasoned melted cheese. The name has been used for various dips, one of the most important being fondue bourguignonne in which raw meat is dipped and cooked in hot oil.

Gates Markers for ski races, formed by poles with flags.

Glacier River of ice formed by snow under pressure at low temperatures.

Glühwein A hot spice wine drink. Can be made with either red or white wine.

Gondola Small cable car holding up to four people. Skis can be attached to the outside of the car. Several cars may be on the running cable at the same time.

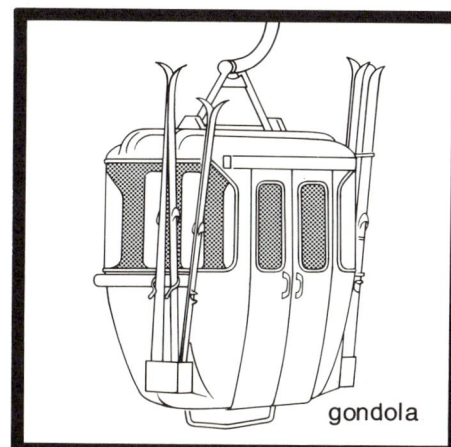

gondola

Herringbone Name given to one method of climbing a hill on skis. The name is derived from the pattern left in the snow.

Igloo Building made from blocks of snow. Usually circular in shape.

Kandahar Club Club founded in 1924 in Murren, Switzerland, to promote downhill skiing and racing. The membership is mainly British.

Luge One or two man toboggan used in races.

Mogul Bumps formed on ski runs by skiers turning on the same place and pushing the snow into a pile.

Mogul slope Practice ski slope consisting of a moving sloping belt.

Piste Ski trail, usually made specially by a machine with rollers.

Puck Used instead of a ball in ice hockey. Disc shaped and made of vulcanised rubber.

Rake Toothed edge at the end of a skate blade used to assist stopping when skating.

Relay Cross country ski race for teams of skiers.

Schussing Straight downhill running without breaking.

Shuttlecock tie Tie decorated with shuttlecocks, worn by Cresta riders who have crashed off the run at Shuttlecock corner.

Sit spin Spin in figure skating. Skater goes into sitting position.

Skeleton Specially designed one-man toboggan made from steel and used only on the Cresta run.

Skibob Framework with seat and steering bar built on to a ski. The ski is in two sections.

Ski-doo Lightweight one-man snowmobile.

Skins Originally seal skins. Strapped to the soles of skis to assist in climbing steep slopes.

Skip Captain of a curling team.

Ski wax Wax used on the soles of skis to help running. Various grades of wax are made for different snow conditions. Wax has now been largely replaced by plastic ski soles.

Slalom Twisting downhill ski course.

Stem Operation of forcing the skis into a V by pressing the heels outwards. Used as the basis of stopping and some turns.

T-bar Particular form of ski lift by which the skiers are pulled up the hill supported by an upside down T-section.

Tail Back part of the ski.

Telemark Region of Norway where one of the older ski turns originated.

Thermostats Temperature operated switches used in ice rinks and other applications.

Tip Front section of the ski.

Tracing Lines in the ice made by skater when doing compulsory figures.

Troika Russian sleigh drawn by three horses running abreast.

Upright spin Spin in figure skating. Skater spins in an upright position.

Water sensor Device used in an ice rink to start the freezing unit if too much water is formed on the surface of the ice.

Wedel or wedeln Set of parallel turns done one after the other.

Index

Numbers in heavy type refer to illustrations

Illustration credits

Photographs

British Tourist Authority
Colour Library International
J. Allan Cash
Fred Dean
Tony Duffy
Mary Evans Picture Library
Food and Agricultural
    Organization
Ronald Grant
Tom Hanley
John Leigh
Mansell Collection
Rob McIntyre
Chichester Ski School
Michigan Tourist Council
Norwegian National Tourist
    Office
Scottish Tourist Board
Snow Institute
Swiss National Tourist Office

Artists
Allard Design Group
Marilyn Day
Ron Hayward Art Group
Illustra Design Ltd
Eric Jewell Associates
B. L. Kearley Ltd
Tony Payne
Rogers & Co.
Peter Sackett Publishing
    Services Ltd